hillside
LANDSCAPING

By Hazel White and the Editors of Sunset Books, Menlo Park, California

PHOTOGRAPHY CREDITS

DESIGN CREDITS

SUNSET BOOKS
VICE PRESIDENT, GENERAL MANAGER
Richard A. Smeby
VICE PRESIDENT, EDITORIAL DIRECTOR
Bob Doyle
DIRECTOR OF OPERATIONS
Rosann Sutherland
MARKETING MANAGER
Linda Barker
ART DIRECTOR
Vasken Guiragossian
SPECIAL SALES
Brad Moses

STAFF FOR THIS BOOK
MANAGING EDITOR
Sally W. Smith
COPY EDITOR
Phyllis Elving
PHOTO EDITOR
Cynthia Del Fava
ILLUSTRATOR
Rik Olson
PRODUCTION SPECIALIST
Linda M. Bouchard
PAGE PRODUCTION
Carrie Davis, Janie Farn,
Susan Paris
PREPRESS COORDINATOR
Eligio Hernandez
PROOFREADER
Michelle Pollace
INDEXER
Nanette Cardon/IRIS

For additional copies of *Hillside Landscaping*
or any other Sunset book, visit us at
www.sunsetbooks.com or call 1-800-526-5111.

COVER
Photo by Saxon Holt; garden design by
Huettl-Thuilot Associates; cover design
by Vasken Guiragossian.

contents

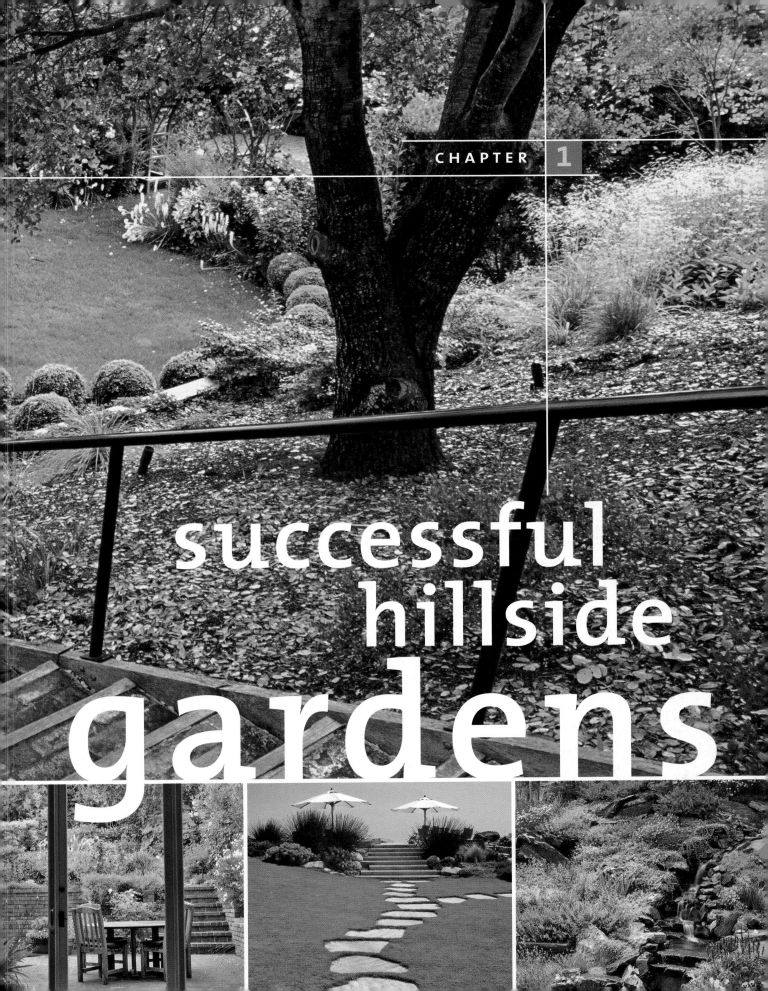

successful hillside gardens

THE PLEASURES OF HILLSIDES

A HILLSIDE GARDEN PROVIDES AN EXPERIENCE OF TOPOGRAPHY— wherever you are in the garden, you are aware of how high you have climbed and how things look from there. Successful hillside gardens draw us pleasurably up and down, making us alert to the land on which we live.

The Lay of the Land

The landscapes that we admire in nature are compositions of vertical and horizontal. Extreme contrasts of the two—a patch of valley floor between towering mountains, a single butte rising from a desert plain— are awe inspiring and mysteriously compelling. Gentle inclines and rolling forms like foothills and grasslands, on the other hand, evoke a calmer sort of pleasure. The interplay of horizontal and vertical is what we draw on in building a hillside garden.

Vertical is exciting, dramatic. Successful gardens on a hillside call attention to the rise of the land with vertical elements such as tall pots, walls, stairways, and trees. Placed toward the top of a slope, these features make the land seem to rise still higher, even straight up to the sky.

Horizontal is soothing, meditative. Arriving at a flat space in a hillside garden, one pauses and takes in the view from that elevation. Great hillside gardens include many such places—a platform at the hilltop with a chair, perhaps, or a boardwalk that floats over the slope—as well as larger level areas for entertaining.

Invitation to Explore

A hillside garden generates curiosity: what's uphill, what's downhill, guests wonder. The top of the garden is the preferred destination (see pages 62–63). We like to be up on top of the world looking out, even if it's only 15 feet up and the view doesn't quite clear the roof. There's still a different perspective to be gained from there.

The most memorable hillside gardens have carefully choreographed ascents to the top. In essence, the journey is a pilgrimage toward the light. A designer might arrange the climb so that the view is blocked at first and the path takes you through tall plantings, with only glimpses of light through the foliage. But you walk on, anticipating the light, until suddenly the view opens before you and you stand bathed in sunlight.

The bottom of the hill (pages 64–65) has an altogether different character. One anticipates shadows downhill and a chill in the air. Going

down, we experience a loss of perspective but also sense the possibility of shelter—from the wind, and also from the myriad stimulations of daily life. If the top of the hill is an exhilarating place, the bottom of the hill is for privacy and reflection.

A New Perspective

Some hillside gardens provide a panorama of ocean or valley, but in metro-politan and suburban areas what you see is quite likely to be only a squint of a natural feature, or a bird's-eye view into the street. Whatever your view,

though, it's worth promoting. It's pleasant to be perched above the neighborhood watching a bicyclist go by or children as they head home from school. Maybe a monument across town is lit at night, or clouds come rolling in from the north, or rooftops make a pleasing pattern—seats that offer up such scenes are bound to be popular resting places.

Besides the view out beyond your garden's boundaries, a hillside garden can afford rewarding sights within your property as well. One of the most dear will be of the house itself, settled into the land, as you see it from above or below. It registers as home, as the place one returns to—a very particular place right here, with the land embracing it just so.

Watercourses

In a sloping garden, water features are immediately credible. They evoke scenes in nature of water draining downhill through the soil or over it, forming springs, creeks, waterfalls, and ponds. Situated more or less as they appear in nature, with a pond at the base of the slope and a spring on high ground or pouring from a bank, such features can create the garden's central narrative.

Designers like to create views of the water and provide areas where you can get close enough to touch it or to tramp along

mossy banks. The sound of the water will change according to the lay of the land; it will rush noisily through a chasm and then murmur across a barely sloping lawn. Paths and stopping places will position you to notice each part of the water's journey, including the spot where dogwood blossoms collect or butterflies bathe in the mud. Children, of course, will float paper boats over the falls.

Thrill-Seeking

Hillside gardens are for heroes—you know there's information to be gained by exploring the site, leaving the comfort of the house to adventure to the top or descend downhill.

Great hillside gardens make the most of the possibilities for adventure and thrill. A path might pass close to a cliff edge (safely, of course) or land you on a log at the top of a waterfall without any railing to help you across. The journey might take in dark thickets of foliage, posing in your imagination the possibility of getting lost, or a pool that seems to drift into infinity at its far edge. When you find your way back to the house, you'll have a fresh experience of the meaning of home.

How to Use This Book

Check out the Guide to Design on the following pages and the gardening chapter on pages 136–159 for ideas that seem pertinent to your own site. Trust your eyes to do the work at this stage, and then walk the garden to try to envision how you might incorporate the ideas that have caught your attention.

Once your plan feels solid, refer to the construction guidelines in Chapter 3 and Chapter 4 to get a sense of what you can build yourself and what you might save for a contractor. Keep in mind that it's not expensive materials that will make your hillside beautiful, but carrying out your own particular vision of a vivid garden experience, using the concepts presented in this book.

guide to design

HILLSIDE GARDENS PRESENT MORE DESIGN OPPORTUNITIES
THAN FLAT ONES. THE NATURAL TOPOGRAPHY GIVES
YOU LICENSE TO DESIGN A TINY SCRAMBLING PATH,
A VINE-COVERED PATIO TUCKED INTO THE SLOPE, OR
AN EXHILARATING HILLTOP SPACE OPEN TO THE VIEW
AND THE SKY. YOU CAN ALSO SHAPE THE LAY OF THE
LAND INTO BEAUTIFUL BANKS AND WATERCOURSES.

ENTRANCE AREAS

THE BEST ENTRYWAY GARDENS ARE CHOREOGRAPHED CROSSINGS FROM PUBLIC TO PRIVATE SPACE. To help guests experience a sense of glad arrival, start your welcome right at the street. Plan every step to the front door so that people will arrive relaxed and already charmed by your hospitality.

BELOW: **Wood, pebbles, stone paving, and plants create a vivid textural experience—and different sounds underfoot—as you walk from street to door. There's rhythm built into the experience: first the stairs, then a jog to the left between screens of horsetail** (Equisetum hyemale), **and then pavers of various sizes that make you improvise your pace as you go (or hopscotch along if you have the urge). Pictured from both the street (below) and the house (inset), the entrance is an apt introduction to the particular qualities of this property—all the materials are repeated in other garden spaces as well.**

Place a solid stone apron at the doorstep if your entrance path is gravel. It will help keep gravel from traveling into the house on people's shoes.

ABOVE: Poured-concrete steps seeded with small pebbles zigzag around planting spaces filled with lavender. The stairway's predictability—three steps and a rest, three steps and a rest—and the many pathside lights make tripping unlikely.

RIGHT: A shaded entranceway can be uninviting and may raise fears about safety. Prune or thin trees to allow some light to fall on the path, and do whatever you can to make the area at the front door open and sunlit. People will gladly walk through shadows—even linger to enjoy the light flickering on leaves—as long as they can see sunlight ahead. Imagine the difference in the atmosphere if the gate shown here were a solid barrier.

LEFT: Plan an entry garden so there is beauty all year. For a city house, the planting scheme might be formal; in a more natural setting, as here, an informal massing of plants that change through the seasons works well. These plantings are lavish in scale but low, allowing a full view of the front door.

BELOW: The passage through the trees to this house on the crest of a hill is almost ceremonial, as if you are walking through an arcade of columns. The approach is purposefully drawn out so that you arrive slowly, strolling through dappled shadows to rise once and then again toward the house and the light. Note the generous width of the walkway and the gracious dimensions of the Italian tile steps: tiny risers, deep treads. The steps are probably unnecessary for such a mild slope, but they extend the color and horizontal lines of the house, doubling its scale and making it feel quite grand.

If a path to the garden runs off the approach to your home's entryway, use a different paving material; for example, you might switch from elegant cut stone to gravel or bark mulch for the garden path. Then visitors will not be confused about the way to the front door.

ABOVE LEFT: If your front door isn't visible from the street, you must present a strong visual clue (or several clues) to let new visitors know where it is. Here, the large white arbor draped with wisteria leaves no doubt. Under the arbor, there's a spacious area for people to linger comfortably over good-byes without backing into one another down the steps. The steps blend with the plant-covered walls as if to de-emphasize the climb, and your eye scales them instantly, darting from bronze foliage to bronze foliage.

ABOVE RIGHT: An entryway gate helps secure a property from intruders, but it is also an opportunity to mark the garden threshold in a special way. This gate doubles as a kinesthetic sculpture, pivoting in its arching frame as you enter.

PATIOS AND DECKS

PATIOS AND DECKS INVITE YOU TO LIVE A LITTLE IN THE OPEN AIR. A large one close to the house is a luxury on a hillside— a patio may need to be dug out of the slope or a deck raised off the ground—but it's a sensible investment to make, because the outdoors becomes usable then. Easier to organize are small patios and decks along the garden paths—stopping places to admire the plantings, or to hide from the sound of the phone.

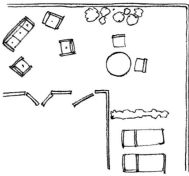

Wrap a deck around the house, separating it into different areas that correspond to the adjoining indoor rooms.

BELOW LEFT: A patio off a guest bedroom generously provides a private place to enjoy the view. The architecture contrasts deliberately with the natural surroundings, like a sculpture set down in the woods.

BELOW RIGHT: Decking suits a range of garden and architectural styles, contemporary to rustic. The only place it's not right is with a formal European-style house.

Saving the Forests

Until recently, the woods of choice for decking were the best grades of redwood and cedar, which generally come from the oldest trees. But now, to protect natural forests, some environmentally sensitive designers are opting to use plantation-grown woods or lumber from certified forests. Wood-polymer composites are another option; waterproof and splinter free, they can be painted or stained, cut and drilled like standard lumber.

ABOVE: From inside, this residence feels like an elegant treehouse, with the fronds of the surrounding Phoenix palms almost entering the top two floors. On warm evenings, the owners slide the doors open and watch foxes, coyotes, hawks, and falcons in the canyon below. The decks' cable railings are visually unobtrusive.

Sitting Places

Finding space for seating on hillside paths may require some ingenuity. One option is to set a seat right into the hillside or to make a retaining wall double as a seat. Or consider placing a chair at the end of a path, widening the path a little there if you can.

ABOVE: This elegant, spacious-looking cut-stone patio was an upgrade from a cramped concrete one. New stone and stucco retaining walls replaced unsightly old wooden ones; raised planting beds and a fireplace were added. The designers cut into the bank to make room for it all.

ABOVE: Patio furniture is a matter of personal style—but also whether the legs will get stuck or wobble on the paving. Airy furniture was a great choice here; blocky wood chairs and table would have eaten up the space. And this paving suits the slender feet. Mortar the gaps between bricks or stone paving units or choose furniture with broad feet that span the gaps.

BELOW: A perfect deck for outdoor living is directly off the kitchen, so you can walk over the threshold into the fresh air without thinking, your coffee in hand. It could be a small space, but it must be comfortable—exposed to gentle breezes if your climate is hot, sheltered against the house if your climate is cool.

ABOVE: This breakfast patio was carved out of the bank in a shape that corresponds to the bow window, the curves of the land, and the paths. Bougainvillea planted above the retaining wall spills over and almost hides it. Notice the absence of tall shrubs; the low plantings show off the shape of the land and the forms of the trees.

RIGHT: As a rule of thumb, you'll need at least 20 square feet of decking to comfortably accommodate each person—that's 80 square feet for a grouping of four—plus space for furniture and any other items. The benches built into this deck can also hold trays of food and drinks. If the deck is some distance from the house, you might install a seat that doubles as a storage unit for cushions and candles.

LEFT: On a hillside property, it's possible to spend much of your time off the ground. You can wrap decks around the house walls, providing comfortable places to sit at different times of day as well as both sunny and shady spots for planters. And you can even make a separate retreat by building an extra deck away from the house in the treetops, or facing out to a view. The deck under the trees here is reached by a boardwalk nestled behind the foreground shrubs.

ABOVE: Decks create distinct stopping places along the path through this wooded hillside garden near Seattle. One is sited to catch a view out through the Douglas firs; another makes a platform for a hundred-year-old teak *joglo* (Javanese house), cantilevering over a koi pond.

OPPOSITE BOTTOM: A private place away from the house with its own ceiling (near left) or walls and windows (far left) allows for fantasy—one might live more simply here, tell time by the movement of the sun, restore oneself by writing or sleeping. The path to such a retreat could be long or steep to emphasize the sense of isolation.

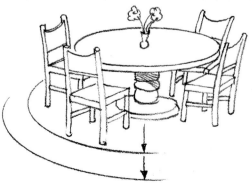

Allow 4½ feet of clearance all around an outdoor dining table. The more room there is, the more gracious the space will feel.

LAWNS

A LAWN MAY ROLL PLEASINGLY WITH A HILLSIDE'S NATURAL TOPOGRAPHY OR stretch out along a perfectly flat terrace cut into the hill, where it will be easier to mow and maintain. Either way, a lawn provides a luxurious surface that's restful to the eye. People are so comfortable on a grassy area that they will lie down on it to gaze at the sky, and even sleep there. Lawn is the best surface for play, too.

For a formal look, keep the lawn on fairly flat terraces separated by steps.

OPPOSITE: The landscape-timber risers of this staircase are like a stream between banks of lawn, drawing particular attention to the undulating topography. Much fun can be had shaping and modeling lawns on slopes: flat, geometric terraces create formality and provide contrast to unterraced areas; flowing shapes and a little sculpting, with both mown and unmown grass as shown here, can emphasize a site's natural beauty.

BELOW: A lawn creates a clearing among the trees on this knoll; the grass appears to fall away at the edges into the understory plantings. Spaces where gardens meet the natural landscape can have a particular poignancy, bringing into focus our relationship to the beauty around us. The play between the natural and the constructed is especially lovely here, and this lawn a perfect place to walk into the shade and out again into the light, thinking.

BELOW: A healthy, neatly mown green lawn provides an attractive foreground for a house and a pleasing contrast to the riot of color and textures in a flower garden. Running lawn through garden spaces can do away with the need for paths; place stepping-stones or a pad of paving in spots that receive the most traffic.

RIGHT: A flat carpet of lawn near the house provides a practical outdoor living space. Tables and chairs can be set up for social gatherings, children can roll balls over the grass or place a paddling pool there. Landscape designers often cut into a hillside that slopes down to a house in order to create such an area.

PATHS

PATHS PLAY A VITAL ROLE IN ANY HILLSIDE GARDEN. THEY MUST BE SO INVITING AND offer such enchantment that visitors are willing to leave the comfort of the house and level ground to climb the slope. Even if your garden falls away from the house, visitors will need to be lured downhill because of the prospect of the walk back up.

OPPOSITE: To draw people uphill, create a desirable-looking resting place at the end of each stretch of the path. Spotlight it by framing it through an arch or setting it between a pair of shrubs. Place a fragrant rose alongside a bench, or arrange the seat so that it offers a view. The ascent through a garden can be staged so that each resting spot is pleasurable in a different way.

BELOW: Shadowy stretches of path are sometimes inevitable on a hill. Pay attention to such spots; they present the possibility of creating a special sense of shelter and privacy. One might linger against a tall, cool stone wall (right), out of sight of neighbors or the house, or enjoy a daydream of being lost amid exuberant foliage (left). The garden-maker's care dispels any sense of gloom—Italian cypresses point the way out into sunlight; a giant glass bauble glows with light.

Have a path meander over, between, under, alongside, and around other garden elements to slow the journey through the garden.

LEFT: To prevent people from rushing along a comfortable path, arrange to catch their attention. Here, for example, a stream is hidden in the foliage, but the bridge and the rhododendron plantings (multiple visual clues often are necessary) extend an invitation to stop and find the water.

BELOW: Be decisive about the purpose of your paths. For convenience, you may need a path to go straight from the house to the parking area; it should be wide and safe to walk quickly. On the other hand, a path that takes in the topography, leading you to the garden's secret places, should invite slowness and even provide boulders on which to sit. It's not inconvenient that such a path curve this way and that, or that plants flop over it.

ABOVE: Tiny trails promise adventure. You might clear one through a meadow, letting it dip and rise with the terrain and even steering it toward rabbit holes and anthills. Don't avoid damp or even muddy areas; lay a few stepping-stones and people will enjoy picking their way across. These flowers are calliopsis *(Coreopsis tinctoria)*, sun-loving annuals grown from seed.

ABOVE: Fragrance will stop people in their tracks. It could take all of a pleasant afternoon to make your way through a hillside garden with paths like this. Roses arch from the bank at a convenient height for inhaling their scent; chamomile between the stepping-stones releases its fragrance as you walk on it.

BELOW: Use sunlight to pull people through the garden; we love light and will walk toward it without much urging. Keep at least a partial view of the sky open; don't block it with thick shrubbery. If necessary, thin trees so that light filters through and the sky shows the way ahead.

Place stepping-stones so they relate to one another. Set the straight edge of one stone against a straight edge of another; place a concave edge against a convex edge.

STEPS AND STAIRWAYS

STEPS CREATE A SERIES OF HORIZONTAL LINES UP A HILLSIDE GARDEN; they make a strong design element, and if they are well designed they are inviting to climb. Where the grade gets steep, create landings between short flights of stairs to give people plenty of excuses to pause.

ABOVE: Well-designed steps draw you onto them. Here, the bottom steps are wide, spilling onto the patio so you can't ignore them. Sooner or later, you'll accept the invitation to see where they go.

LEFT: The horizontal lines of the steps play an important role in this garden. They introduce a spirit of calmness and peg the liveliness of the plantings to the ground so that one feels a real sense of place. The plant forms are seen to good advantage from below.

RIGHT: Small plants growing in the joints between risers and treads soften the appearance of steps and give them charm. Although some plants, such as thyme, can be trodden on without damage, keep them trimmed so there's no chance anyone will slip when plants are wet.

For drama, run steps straight up and down a slope. For an easier climb and to draw out the journey, zigzag the steps across the slope.

LEFT: As you design your steps, consider how they will look from above—the tread shapes, the edge angles, the pattern of materials. Contrasting risers and treads, like these, help you discern the step edges as you descend, reducing the chance of stumbling when steps are steep. The gravel treads flow into the gravel path and the timber risers match the retaining wall, de-emphasizing the staircase as a separate element.

A single step composed of two large slabs of rock breaks the downhill flow of a steep gravel path. To prevent tripping when there's only one step, make it so bold it cannot be missed.

ABOVE: These steps in a rocky hillside garden could almost have been carved out of bedrock. The sharp edges are hidden in mats of thyme, and the steps jog this way and that to avoid a spill of boulders. Varied riser widths make pleasing lines, and the boulders are just the right height for sitting.

ABOVE: A wooden staircase bridges a bank, keeping strollers' feet out of the mud and grass seed off their shoes—and protecting the bank from erosion. This is a simple solution for difficult terrain, leaving a natural space like this meadow free of hardscape.

OPPOSITE: When a small, steep site makes it impossible to build steps graciously wide and shallow, with landings to let visitors catch their breath, you'll need to work extra hard to make the steps inviting. Color animates this stairway, and wood extensions to the concrete steps conjure up a sense of roominess. The slim handrail and recessed lighting are space-efficient details. There's even room for plants; despite the constraints of the site, this is a generous-seeming space.

BELOW: The rule of thumb for an inviting and easy climb is five steps per flight of stairs—more may daunt your visitors, fewer earn extra graciousness. In both examples below, the paving matches the site's natural stone; using a single material for step risers, treads, and adjoining paths creates an elegant, understated style. The honey-colored stairs at left are made of concrete cut to look like stone; they have an energetic swing to them, as if they could almost lift you up the hill.

RETAINING WALLS

THE PRACTICAL REASON FOR BUILDING A RETAINING WALL IS TO HOLD STEADY A BANK OF SOIL. Just as important, though, is the sense of shelter and comfort a wall provides. A wall embraces a space and separates it from the rest of the world. The word "paradise," in fact, derives from a Persian word meaning "a walled place."

OPPOSITE TOP: A stone wall appears enduring, immediately giving a new garden a settled look. This granite wall, curving and rising with the shape of the land, could be here for centuries. The seats will be smooth and dipped by then.

BELOW: A tall retaining wall can loom over a small patio. One way to lessen the impact is to step the wall down into a terrace and then a smaller wall. Here, plants soften both walls; it's a good idea to leave a planting space at the foot of a wall. The purple-flowered plants are fragrant heliotrope.

Plant a tree near a high retaining wall so that the shadows of its branches and leaves will soften and break up the face of the wall.

RIGHT: For stability, a dry-stacked stone wall needs to slant back into the bank about 2 inches for each foot of height; slanting it more, like this, is a matter of style. Note the boldness of this wall, with its massive stones, deeply shadowed horizontal spaces, and strong color. The sweeps of tall ornamental grasses are an excellent match for the wall.

RIGHT: If you are planning a patio wall, consider a fireplace to make the space warm, welcoming, and comfortable in all but the most wintry weather. This chimney clad in terra-cotta celebrates the site's vertical nature, soaring up the hillside. Consult your local building inspector to find out setback and chimney height requirements, and install a spark arrester to prevent large embers from escaping.

ABOVE: This tall wall a few yards from the back of the house captures attention in several ways: water spills from a ram's head and splashes into a canal recessed in the patio floor; vines and side plantings make a bower for a bench; and a flight of steps without a rail leaps in an arc over the canal, promising adventure as you journey into the garden above.

LEFT: Poured-concrete walls reinforced with steel at the core can be made slim, like these. If space is tight, choosing a concrete wall may allow you to step it down into two walls, creating a terrace for citrus trees and trailing rosemary that will fill the area with fragrance.

Cap a low retaining wall to create a bench and invite people to sit among the flowers. A height of about 18 inches is comfortable.

RIGHT: Good choices for a cottage garden above a wall are patches of creeping thyme and other plants that prefer good drainage (including most rock-garden plants—see pages 152–155). At the base of a dry-stacked wall, where moisture from the soil behind will seep through, find places for ferns and other moisture-loving plants.

RIGHT: Landscape architect and sculptor Jack Chandler bought a batch of steel plates to recycle as structural elements in his garden in Napa Valley, California. The sheets were 36 inches tall, a convenient height for retaining walls on either side of a walkway that zigzags up the hillside. Cut into strips, the metal worked as risers for the steps, too.

PLANTING BEDS AND TERRACES

YOU CAN GARDEN ON A SLOPE, BUT IT'S A LOT EASIER ON THE LEVEL—especially if you grow vegetables or flowering plants, which need regular care. Frame your terraces as you please, with formal brick or stone, more casual wood boards, or even crates filled with recycled objects.

LEFT: A terrace frame needs to be sufficiently sturdy to hold back the weight of the soil behind it, which can be considerable when the soil is wet. But the material for the frame need not be conventional—these gabions are filled with recycled clay building supplies, including bricks, tiles, pipes, and flowerpots. Careful attention has been paid to the stacking of the objects.

OPPOSITE: Stone walls embrace planting beds and retain gently sloping terraces of lawn. This is a formal, architectural space appropriate for a grand home—the walls are clean-edged, straight, and regularly spaced; the lawn is manicured and more or less geometrically shaped. But it's a relaxed formality; the trees are not on a grid, and the plantings are informal. One might wander contentedly here, stopping to smell the roses or rest on a warm wall end.

A long arbor on a terrace can be planted with vines or climbing roses.

ABOVE: The horizontal run of these formal terraces plays against the vertical nature of the site. For the most drama, emphasize both axes. Wall pots, wall buttresses, a straight-up-the-hill staircase, slim Italian cypresses, and mature trees near the house all add height to this scene. The horizontal is accentuated by distinct wall edges, long strips of a single kind of plant, and a flat gravel walkway.

LEFT: The opposite of a formal terrace is one that curves with the hillside, maybe stopping where the slope is mild and starting up again as necessary, the whole enterprise intermittently smothered with plantings. A pleasing sense of order is introduced here in the restrained use of color, primarily chartreuse, yellow, and scarlet.

LEFT: These planting beds are not much larger than window boxes, but they pack a lot of color onto a very steep site. Note the pretty detailing at the tops of the walls; if terraces lie close to formal architecture, give the frames a fanciful touch and they'll look handsome even before any flowers bloom.

RIGHT: For a vegetable garden, which typically needs regular work, it may make sense to zigzag a path between raised beds so that you can access plants easily from more than one side. Design the beds and any trellises to be attractive from both above and below, even when empty; have fun arranging crop patterns. If you will be reaching in to sow seeds, apply mulch, and weed, each bed should be no more than an arm's length from edge to center, or about 4 feet in total width.

LEFT: Before a remodel, this garden was a formal arrangement of lawn and roses; now it's relaxed and softly flowing. Drifts of lavender, ornamental grasses, pride of Madeira *(Echium fastuosum),* rockrose *(Cistus),* and other unthirsty plants fill the wall-framed terraces. The walls descend the slope in long sections, providing calm and elegant lines against the sweep of plants.

These terraces braced with concrete walls step down the slope almost like rice fields. A warm tint was added to the concrete mix, which was poured in frames made of cedar shakes to add texture. Some of the terraces are devoted to perennial plantings, while a river of gray slate runs through some and still others showcase seasonally changing vegetables and herbs. The view of the terraces from above is striking—see page 63.

Raised planting beds alongside a flight of steps are fine sites for fragrant plants like this Burmese honeysuckle (*Lonicera hildebrandiana*) spreading against the wall. Yellow-flowered kangaroo paw (*Anigozanthos*) and burgundy New Zealand flax (*Phormium*) provide a striking but easily maintained arrangement of forms and colors the year around.

To create a unified look, incorporate stairs made of lumber into terraces framed with landscape timbers.

BANKS

A BANK THAT HAS ATTRACTIVE CONTOURS— PERHAPS GRADED—CAN BE PLANTED WITH LOW, HUGGING GROUND COVER TO PLAY UP ITS SHAPE. Wildflowers or native plants might be used to emphasize the character of a naturalistic bank (one with a swale running through it, for example). Sometimes the topography of a bank is not especially attractive; then you can disguise it with an undulating cover of shrubs. There are many ways to make banks beautiful.

BELOW LEFT: This dynamically sculptural home sits on a bank dotted with curvaceous silvery blue agaves—striking architectural forms keeping company with remarkable forms of nature. Before you plant a bank at a house entrance, check that the plants will show the house to best advantage; note the silhouettes of the agaves seen against this house from the driveway and the low planting that lets the bank serve as a simple plinth for the display of the architecture.

BELOW: Pieces of architectural salvage lie like temple ruins amid the undergrowth on this bank, introducing a sense of narrative— where did the pieces come from, and who engraved the hands in the stone? It's a stopping place for a flight of fantasy. And the architectural lines and texture of the stone set off the plantings beautifully.

Make a ledge garden by setting stone slabs firmly into a bank. A mat-forming plant will mask the gap between two small slabs.

ABOVE: A riot of color on a bank becomes particularly beautiful if there's some order to it—the eye loves to discern similarities as well as differences. Here, the flowering shrubs are evergreen Kurume hybrid rhododendrons (with small, glossy leaves and a profusion of small flowers) and deciduous Exbury hybrid azaleas (growing to 6 feet tall, with later-blooming flowers up to 5 inches across, sometimes ruffled or fragrant). One could linger here, pleased to be able to name this as a distinct place: a rhododendron dell.

INSET: Boulders and large sweeps of grasses on sloping ground read as natural landscape; it's as if the grasses have swayed in the wind over these stones for centuries. Of course, they have been chosen for their late-summer color, to harmonize with one another and with the lavender and the dark purple New Zealand flax (Phormium) in the background.

LEFT: In nature, an open hillside is often colonized by wildflowers. A perfect mix for a garden bank includes wildflowers that bloom at different times, some at least into fall. To avoid sowing new seed each year, create a mix of self-sowing annuals and perennials suited to your site (for example, moisture- and sun-loving). Growing here are gloriosa daisies *(Rudbeckia hirta)*, Queen Anne's lace *(Daucus carota)*, and daylilies *(Hemerocallis)*.

OPPOSITE TOP: At the shore's edge, banks of ornamental grasses and flowering shrubs border a lawn that rolls smoothly and gently, echoing the ocean surface on a calm day. Bank plantings absorb the drop-off to the shore and establish another soft horizontal line, low enough that you can see the ocean beneath the tree canopies. Access to the shoreline involves passing through this buffer zone between clipped and "civilized" open space and the wild water. As the tall grasses brush your legs, you might be tempted to pull off your shoes and head barefoot to the water's edge.

Settle a boulder so that its widest part is even with the top of the surrounding soil.

LEFT: 'Rose Glow' Japanese barberry *(Berberis thunbergii)* puts a shock of rich pink on this bank in early autumn. After the leaves drop, bright red beadlike berries stud the branches throughout the winter. New leaves in spring are marbled bronzy red and pinkish white. Alongside a Japanese barberry, consider growing low heaths and heathers; they come in a range of foliage colors, with flower colors from white to lavender and purple. For other good plant choices for banks, see pages 146–151.

RIGHT: Where a path runs through, a bank may need some buttressing. Instead of building a formal retaining wall, one option is to push boulders into the slope. The dark red barberry *(Berberis)* in the foreground was chosen to match the striations in the stones; the yellow poppies harmonize with the stones' warm tones.

ROCK GARDENS

A ROCK GARDEN NEEDS STONES AND PLANTS PROPORTIONED and arranged to call forth the image of a high alpine meadow, scree, or rocky out-cropping. The plants themselves need not be true alpines; as long as they look the part, they can be lowland plants that thrive in ordinary gardens.

To make a natural-looking composition using a large, rounded rock, add a reclining rock and a flat rock—all three shapes are placid and peaceful.

BELOW: Naturally rocky gardens need only a little staging to show them off. Take paths close to the rock faces so people can touch the stone, and keep the plantings low to ensure that the bedrock or any loose rock that's tumbled from a nearby outcrop will show through. Echeveria and sedum have colonized this rocky slope.

ABOVE: The quintessential alpine plant is a low-growing, gemlike species that can survive against the odds in thin, gravelly soil. Succulents are a different breed, but because they are frequently small, exquisitely decorative, and able to thrive in harsh-looking conditions, they make good substitutes in mild climates. Red-tinged flapjack plant *(Kalanchoe thyrsiflora)* and blue chalksticks *(Senecio mandraliscae)* grow where they can between the stones of this garden.

RIGHT: Low-growing fragrant pinks *(Dianthus)* and stonecress *(Aethionema)* make a pretty picture in this rocky scree. Gravel and boulders are pleasingly matched; choose stone native to your region, or do as landscape architects often do and ask for gravel and boulders that came from the same quarry. (See pages 152–155 for other excellent rock-garden plants).

LEFT: The difficulties of incorporating a traditional rock garden into a residential setting are reduced if the home looks like a mountain cabin and the rocks are already a feature of the landscape beyond the garden. To soften transitions to other parts of the garden, carry the colors of the rock garden and some of the same rock into those areas. You might shape and plant a lawn as an alpine meadow and use rocky berms or stands of conifers to hide any elements that jar with the look of the rock garden.

BELOW: The rocks in a rock garden are just as important as the plants. Flat-topped rock like this creates a tranquil scene. The plants are growing as they do in nature, between boulders and in crevices caused by erosion or the freezing and thawing of ice. Consider asking at a stone yard if a large rock can be split into horizontal slabs so you can pack soil and gravel between them for planting.

RIGHT: In spring and early summer, creeping *Veronica liwanensis*, just 2 inches tall, carpets the spaces between these boulders with bright blue blossoms. The large, maplelike leaves of *Heuchera micrantha* 'Palace Purple' in the foreground accent a meadow of soft green thyme. This rock garden serves a practical design purpose: it screens a public walking trail from view. The gravel at the base of the boulders is a detail found in natural rockscapes.

A stone trough placed on a flat-topped boulder or a pile of rocks makes a simple rock garden for a patio or a doorstep.

ABOVE: Stone is utilized quite differently in Japanese rock gardens than in alpine ones. In a Japanese garden, gravel creates the impression of a large surface of water, and low stones read as islands or promontories. A vertical stone with a pointed top makes a focal point on higher ground, suggesting mountains.

RIGHT: These plants—'Robusta' rose (*Rosa rugosa* hybrid), poppy *(Papaver)*, veronica (*Veronica austriaca teucrium* 'Crater Lake Blue'), catmint (*Nepeta* 'Six Hills Giant'), and lamb's ears *(Stachys byzantina)*—are more typically found in a bed of Mediterranean perennials than in a rock garden. But growing in lush clumps among the stones, they have the feel of wildflowers beside a mountain stream.

PLACES FOR POTS

POTS PROVIDE EXTRA SPACE FOR CHOICE PLANTS WHEN A GARDEN IS TOO STEEP TO accommodate many planting beds. There's room for plenty of pots in a hillside garden, not only on a patio or deck but also decorating the tops or bases of walls and the sides of steps. Planted or not, pots can also be positioned to serve as accents at the end of a view, or even plunged into a bank.

LEFT: Containers of roses decorate this sitting area with summer-long blossoms. The most popular flowers in the world, roses symbolize a sense of garden more than any other plant. Here they make an intimate, magical retreat on a ledgelike patio in a steep, wild valley.

OPPOSITE: The beautifully constructed stonework in this garden is a focal point in its own right. The pots draw attention to the stonework, inviting the eye to explore the lines and colors of the stone and the lidded jar. Stage garden compositions with pots, using their colors, lines, and textures as elements in your arrangements.

To call people uphill, place a bubbling water jar at the top of the steps.

ABOVE: Potted plantings at the foot and on top hide this concrete-block wall, or at least draw attention away from the utilitarian blocks. The pots are mostly large and the plants tall; smaller pots are raised up on platforms. The top of the wall is partially obscured by spreading plants growing on the bank. Pots might also have been attached to the face of the wall.

LEFT: Because of the effort needed to walk uphill and down, a hillside garden needs to be full of signs that you are moving in the right direction and headed toward a special place. Vibrant, beautifully planted and maintained pots like these at the top of stairs suggest that the gardener has thought about you and any effort you make will be rewarded.

Vary the height and color of a fence to frame a view or screen an eyesore—or just to be playful.

FENCES

FENCES ARE BUILT TO MARK BOUNDARIES AND DETER intruders, but well-chosen fences also work as design elements in the garden. A fence can support a fragrant vine, flicker with the shadows from a maple tree, or make strong structural lines to match the elegant architecture of a house.

BELOW: Inspired by Japanese torii gates at Shinto shrines, this bamboo fence was designed and built by California furniture maker Paul Henry. The rectangular panels vary in height and width as they step down the hillside; between some pairs of panels are shelves to display ceramic art. Fences can also be built with shelves for bonsai; panels might be metal, recycled wood pieces, or even red-hued acrylic. Consider working with a metal fabricator or a sculptor to create such a structure.

ABOVE: A fence can draw a delightful line through a sloping garden, especially in winter when plants are dormant—or lost under dollops of snow. It announces the shape of the hill by marching down in sections or flowing with the contours (see page 94). As you plan a fence, think about its horizontal lines and the pattern of the panels in relation to the scale and texture of your plantings. Consider what the fence material looks like when wet, and what will be visible through the fence.

ABOVE RIGHT: Chain-link fencing is strong enough to support masses of thick vines, whereas a picket fence might well buckle under the load. There's an ecosystem in this living fence covering, so you can expect to find spiders' webs and hear rustlings.

RIGHT: A lattice fence seems more welcoming than a plain board fence; it reveals something of the garden inside, insists less on privacy. To make a tall fence less imposing, split it into two levels as shown here—where the upper portion of the fence is more open still. Many fences have definite front and back sides, the back revealing the posts and rails, but this one has two "good" sides. For an entrance garden, choose a fence that looks handsome from both sides.

PONDS

A POND MAKES A GRAND ORNAMENT IN A HILLSIDE GARDEN. A world forms on the pond surface: pollen from garden flowers, leaves from a tree up the hillside, pea green algae, a water spider—and glittering reflections of the sky and the garden plantings on the pond banks.

LEFT: Water seems to collect naturally in a sunken area on this hillside, then spill gently downhill into a stream. Design a pond to suit the topography: shallow-looking, wide, and densely planted at the edge of a sloping meadow, or deep and rock-strewn for a steep and rocky site. Here, shadowy water is beautifully mysterious.

OPPOSITE: A large, deep pond uphill from a house can create a frisson of tension; the eye recognizes the possible danger should the bank breach. To counter any subconscious anxiety, use the shape of the pond or streamlike plantings beyond to suggest that the water is flowing in a different direction. Here it seems to be headed into the woods; generous paving also establishes a sense of containment.

A formal reflection pool extends elegantly below a long, straight retaining wall.

ABOVE: Even in a small urban yard, water moves through the soil and collects in pools, so it is entirely feasible and satisfyingly believable that the water in this pond drained from the steep hillside garden; the drainpipe set into the bank speaks to that likelihood. In the same way, the abalone shells and glass balls seem to belong here, adding sparkle and reflected watery images. Moisture-loving plants adorn the concrete pond rim.

LEFT: Flat spaces are crucial in a hillside garden. They provide a place to rest and take in the surroundings, in contrast to the active journeying up and down. Water and the paving surrounding it make a large, still space on this hillside. Although the land drops away to the right, this isn't a precipitous ledge; bounded by trees and ornamental grasses, it is a spot where one could settle peacefully.

WATERFALLS

WATER PLUNGING FROM A ROCKY LEDGE OR SPILLING DOWN IN A SERIES OF CASCADES ANIMATES A HILLSIDE GARDEN with its sound and deepens our appreciation for the character of the garden topography. The sound itself can be enough to draw visitors uphill or down, especially if they are able to glimpse part of the falls or a bridge that crosses the water.

BELOW LEFT: How water travels over a waterfall interests us, so think about directing a path to your falls—otherwise visitors might be tempted to forge one. To design a realistic-looking waterfall, think of the force of a river in spring: boulders might be swept along in its flow, banks flooded, stones worn smooth. Flowers, with their ephemeral connotations, will increase the drama.

BELOW RIGHT: Water, as a basic element of life, summons a sense of reverence. The symbolism is accentuated here by the raised source, the note of formality in the symmetrical plantings at each side of the flagstone water channel, and the straight flow of water to your feet.

This fall of water from the base of a bank makes a lovely water feature in a small space. Insert the spout when you construct the wall, and leave a hole lower in the wall to run tubing to the spout from a pump submerged in the trough.

ABOVE: A waterfall need not be connected to a full-size pond or stream to seem credible. Here, water slips off a spill stone atop a retaining wall as if it had drained from the garden into a marsh of reedy plantings to splash into a rocky cavern beneath the patio floor, the sound reverberating upward.

LEFT: Calm water in a pond mirrors the house architecture and provides a serene setting for a patio. The waterfall is comprised of a series of spill stones, so the water falls and breaks many times, generating a lovely symphony of sound. It makes exquisite background music— but also calls people to leave the comfort of the patio to see just where the water goes.

STREAMS, CREEKBEDS

IN ORDER TO LOOK REAL, A STREAM MUST SEEM TO TAKE THE EASIEST WAY DOWNHILL—following a depression in the land, forming a gorge in a narrow rocky place, wearing away at the outside bank on a turn—until the water spreads into a marsh or tips into a pond at the base of the slope. A natural-looking stream is the most difficult water feature to design in a small garden (see pages 126–127).

OPPOSITE: A moist woodland slope with a rock ledge and a backdrop of untamed landscape is an excellent site for a stream. With so many solid clues to its authenticity, the stream need not be accessible at its source: it might flow from a thicket of alder, willow, or reeds on the edge of the property—and disappear in a similar fashion at the downhill boundary. The less water in the stream, the prettier it will sound, generally, and the more credible it will look.

BELOW: Drifts of moisture-loving, spring-flowering plants signal the presence of water in a swale through a woodland garden. The bridge indicates that in a different season, water might sluice through; you almost sense its motion as you cross over. Bridges are a fine way to experience water; there's a thrill to putting oneself over a flood, even an imagined one.

As you design a dry creekbed, think water: take it around a promontory and past a beach downstream, and place a stepping-stone midstream for the fun of striding offshore.

BELOW: A stone-clad channel collects runoff from the banks on either side and doubles as a watery walkway through the garden. Puddles between the stones sparkle with reflections, breaking up the shade under the trees. Water-loving yellow flag *(Iris pseudacorus)* and plantain lily *(Hosta)* thrive in the wet edges.

RIGHT: This dry creekbed swirls across a sloping lawn, its uphill bank secured with river-washed stones and its pebbly floor dipped as if water really has run through. Blue sea lavender *(Limonium perezii)* stands in for water, the flowers shivering in a breeze. And a clump of wachendorfia hides the end of the creek in a grove of thirsty bamboo.

guide to design 2

CHILDREN'S PLAY SPACES

A HILLSIDE GARDEN CAN PRO-VIDE ENCHANTMENT FOR CHILDREN. It stirs their love of exploration—they'll soon be off looking for experiences up and down the hillside, away from the conversations of adults. You might even consider making places for them to build something to just their scale.

LEFT: Lawn makes a good play surface for games and paddling pools, but wheels go faster on concrete. Edge your lawn with a band of smooth paving to make young drivers happy; when the taxi is jettisoned, the paving can become a runway for a junior pilot. Level lawn makes ball games easier for the whole family, but a steep lawn is excellent for rolling down and racing up.

OPPOSITE: This tree house was the work of the children who play in it as well as a contractor: the contractor built the floor, walls, and roof, and the children created screened-in windows, bunks, and a drawbridge. The most exciting tree houses are high off the ground and far from the house, with a means of access that can be denied to adults.

For the most fun, provide a water supply for sand play—and a boulder for jumping into the moat. To conserve water, fit the faucet with a self-closing valve so water runs only while the tap is held open.

ABOVE: Children need their own space. Let a child choose her own portion of a retaining-wall terrace to grow what she likes, perhaps to stash playthings and tools. For children who prefer wild land to play equipment or gardening, the unmown grass beyond a cultivated area is explorers' territory (top). If the terrain is up and down or rugged, so much the better. You might offer to install a faucet there and provide building materials.

LEFT: Children don't really need steps, except as a surface for tea parties—a slide is much more fun for descending to ground level from a deck. Getting back up the slide is fun, too. Be cautious about a slide on a paved surface; place a thick rubber pad (or a sandbox) at the base of the slide for safety.

TOP OF THE GARDEN

THE TOP OF A HILLSIDE GARDEN IS A SPECIAL PLACE, OFFERING A SENSE OF PROSPECT AND PERSPECTIVE. We are drawn to the spot with the largest view, even if it reveals only a rooftop or the garden just below. As you design the top of your garden, emphasize the sense of its height.

OPPOSITE: Stepping down the hillside, these terraces present a pleasingly flat, quiltlike appearance when viewed from the main patio above. The restful view masks the dizzying drop-off beyond the garden wall. To prevent vertigo, contrast heady experiences of height with views of firm horizontal ground.

BELOW LEFT: People will climb comfortably if the way is sunlit or bathed in a golden aura, like this backlit Japanese maple foliage. Plant your hillside with open-headed, attractively branching trees—oaks, for instance. Or choose trees with thin, quivering leaves or blossoms that will spin light across paths.

BELOW RIGHT: Above your house overlooking the neighborhood is a superior vantage point; you can see farther—a rainstorm coming, the sun rising. You can enjoy a fresh perspective of the house and at the same time enjoy being remote from it.

Angle a seat at the top of the garden toward the best view. For a feeling of comfort, enclose the back side of the seat.

BOTTOM OF THE GARDEN

THE BOTTOM OF A HILLSIDE GARDEN SHOULD HOLD ITS OWN as a distinct place, not just as the point where the slope disappears under the boundary fence. If the house is situated at the base of the slope, it must seem to be holding its own against the slope, too—you don't want dirt running right up to the house wall.

LEFT: Lure visitors down to the bottom of the garden by promising something special. Ceremonial gateways make such an announcement; the reward here is a sunlit grassy bank by a stream at the base of the slope.

OPPOSITE: The bottom of a garden can be particularly cozy because of its sense of shelter. It's a natural spot for a pool, since water accumulates on low ground. Trees and shrubs provide additional comforting enclosure, but make a large clearing at the center of the space for the play of sunlight.

Create a sense of place at the bottom of a garden by carving out a flat area and sheltering it with a tree.

ABOVE: The special place at the bottom of the garden might be out of sight from the house, to seem most like a remote and peaceful refuge. The journey back uphill then becomes a homecoming. Pay attention to framing the house view; if possible, arrange the path so that you walk through shadow and then see home bathed in light.

LEFT: A bank that runs right up to a house wall suggests the force of the hillside, the chance that the earth might slip. Be sure, therefore, to create as large a flat space as you can between the house and the bank, building retaining walls as necessary. If you place furniture there, it shouldn't feel crushed into a narrow corridor. From indoors, the airy blossoming trees are seen in silhouette against the sky.

hillside construction basics

TO BE EXPLORED AND APPRECIATED, GARDENS
MUST HAVE PATHS AND SITTING AREAS; FOR
PRIVACY, THEY NEED FENCES AND GATES. HILLSIDE
GARDENS, HOWEVER, USUALLY ALSO CALL FOR
STEPS AND RETAINING WALLS. IN THIS CHAPTER
YOU'LL LEARN HOW TO BUILD ALL THESE LAND-
SCAPE FEATURES ON A HILLSIDE.

CONTROLLING EROSION AND DRAINAGE

FROM THE BEGINNING OF YOUR LAND-SCAPE PLANNING, AND AT EVERY STEP ALONG THE WAY, consider how to prevent soil erosion and control drainage. Rain-water and snowmelt coursing downhill can take along soil and gradually erode a hill-side garden. Water running rampant across a property could start landslides, break down retaining walls, undermine house foundations, and convert patios into ponds. Once your garden is established, be alert to signs that erosion is developing or that the drainage system needs attention.

A sparsely planted slope is particularly prone to soil erosion. To reduce the chances of that, cover your slope with plants that have dense, strong, spreading roots to hold the soil; see pages 146—151 for plant suggestions.

Indications of Erosion

Even if you don't actually see water washing away your soil, you can detect some signs of erosion fairly easily. Check for any of these conditions:

● TREE ROOTS are exposed (except for species with roots that grow above ground naturally).

● SMALL STONES OR ROCKS that used to be underground have lifted or washed onto the soil surface.

● SMALL GULLIES have formed; often this happens at the base of a slope.

● SILT OR SEDIMENT has built up in low areas or on paths or patios.

Runoff is usually worst where fill soil has been added. Problems can also be anticipated on the downhill side of a large area of paving, particularly if it is impermeable.

If you are new to your property, try this sim-ple test as a clue to how the soil will behave in wet weather. Dig a hole about 2 feet deep (any width) and fill it with water. Let it drain and then fill it again. If it takes hours or even days to drain the second time, or both times, you'll know that most of the water from heavy rain or snowmelt will run off the surface rather than soak in. The steeper the slope, the more severe the runoff—and resulting erosion—will be.

If you suspect a serious erosion problem in your garden (or a problem on a neighbor's property that might impact your own site), seek professional advice from a structural or soils engineer, an erosion control specialist, or an engineering geologist.

Effective Erosion Controls

There are a number of measures you can take to control soil erosion in a hillside garden. Consider the following ways of protecting your slope:

- INSTALL A DRAINAGE SYSTEM that intercepts and reroutes runoff (see pages 70–73).
- CHOOSE GROUND COVERS and shrubs with roots that will thoroughly permeate the soil and foliage that will break the force of falling water; see pages 146–151 for suggested plants. Mulch any bare soil around the plants.
- MAKE SURE ANY IRRIGATION SYSTEM you install is suited to your slope and won't produce streams of runoff (see pages 140–143).
- IF YOU ARE REMODELING or significantly recontouring your garden, preserve as much existing vegetation as possible and do any additional planting as soon as you can after the clearing or grading work. If you can't plant before rains begin, cover the soil with black plastic, making sure that it's in close contact with the soil and well anchored.
- SLOW RUNOFF by placing obstacles in its path, giving the water more time to soak into the ground. The illustration below shows baffles made of landscape timbers set into a hillside to slow runoff. You can also use open or framed terraces, riprap, berms, and retaining walls (see pages 80–87).

BEFORE YOU BUILD

Paving, wall, and pond projects will all affect the drainage patterns on your site. The larger the project—and also the more solid it is—the greater the impact will be. And remember, too, that you need to avoid creating problems for your neighbors.

Determine how you are going to deal with drainage issues before you start any construction. If your hillside has deep gullies, or if energetic streams form with every storm, get professional help with planning and installing a drainage system.

BAFFLES TO CONTROL EROSION

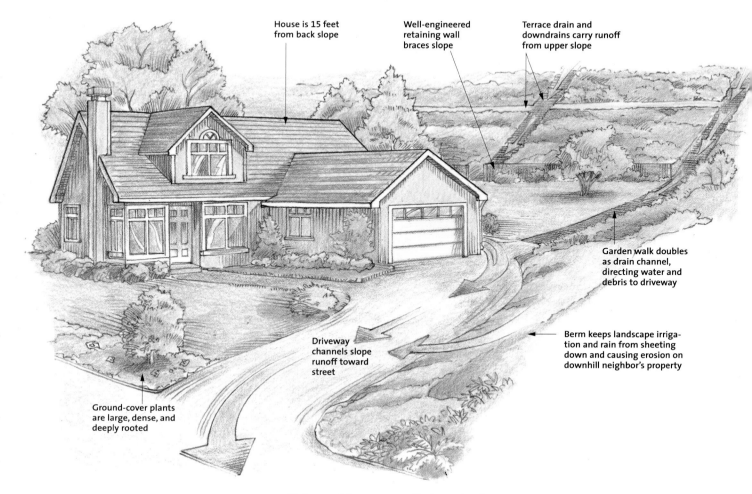

House is 15 feet from back slope

Well-engineered retaining wall braces slope

Terrace drain and downdrains carry runoff from upper slope

Garden walk doubles as drain channel, directing water and debris to driveway

Berm keeps landscape irrigation and rain from sheeting down and causing erosion on downhill neighbor's property

Driveway channels slope runoff toward street

Ground-cover plants are large, dense, and deeply rooted

ABOVE: A hillside property requires a combination of strategies to control erosion. Ideally, the house is at least 15 feet from a back slope, and the hardscape directs runoff away from the house. In the illustration above, horizontal drains on the back slope intercept water and carry it across the slope to drains downhill. A brick path with edges higher than its center doubles as a drain channel, directing water to a sloped driveway. A retaining wall braces the hill, and an 18-inch-high berm prevents runoff from spilling onto the neighbor's property.

Directing and Draining Excess Water

Make a study of the water patterns in your hillside garden. How effective is the existing drainage? Where does runoff flow, and where does water tend to pool? Once you understand the lay of your land, you'll be able to determine how you want to intercept runoff and where you might dispose of it.

Ideally, the soil on your hillside is deep and stable. Rain soaks in, nourishing plantings, or gently drains away or evaporates, causing no trouble. More often, though, at least during a period of heavy rain, water starts to run down the surface of the hillside. Rain may saturate the soil and start to seep out of the slope. Snowmelt can produce surplus water.

Other causes of runoff include poorly planned irrigation, water draining off the roof or paving, and water running off a neighboring property.

You may be able to use erosion control measures (see page 69) to interrupt or reduce the flow of surplus water without installing a drainage system. However, you may need to combine those strategies with surface and sub-surface drains.

Disposal Options

The simplest way to dispose of surplus water is to direct it to an area of the garden where it will not cause a problem—a bed of moisture-loving plants, for example, or a bog garden. Consider using perforated drainpipe to channel the water so that some of it will seep into the soil along the way.

In most cities and suburbs, drainage systems are designed to divert excess water to the street and storm sewers. See the illustration on the facing page for a sense of how to landscape a garden and driveway area to steer water to the street. In outlying or rural areas, you may be able to direct water to a ravine.

Surface drains. Runoff is channeled along the ground by surface drains. Flumes—artificial channels or troughs running down a slope—are one type of surface drain. A dry creekbed can serve as a surface drain in wet weather (see page 127).

ABOVE: This ditch directs runoff to drain the slope; ferns grow in it, and upslope a bridge crosses it.

THREE SURFACE DRAINS

A dry creekbed can be designed to channel water down a slope to a disposal area.

A paved flume with raised edges doubles as a walkway during the dry season.

This bank is drained by a flume of wooden 2 by 12s topped with a grate made of 1 by 1s.

Subsurface drains. Water is carried away underground by subsurface drains. The two main types of subsurface drains are French drains and catch basins.

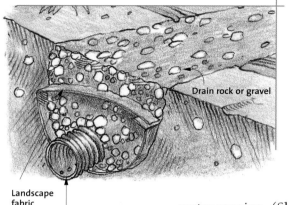

Drain rock or gravel

Landscape fabric

Drainpipe (perforations down)

INSTALLING A FRENCH DRAIN. A French drain is a gravel-filled trench with perforated pipe in the bottom. Water percolates through the gravel into the soil, and the drainpipe routes any excess water to a disposal area.

The trench is typically 2 to 4 feet deep and at least a foot wide. The pipe is a 4-inch perforated drainpipe, capped at the high end; its open end is directed toward a disposal site. If you're installing the drain on a slope, run it parallel to the ground. On flat ground, slope the pipe to keep the water moving. (Slant it downward about 2 percent—a drop of 2 feet for every 100 feet, or about $2^{1/2}$ inches for every 10 feet.)

To install a French drain, follow these steps:

1 **DIG THE TRENCH** and line it with landscape fabric to keep soil from clogging the drainpipe holes, making sure there's enough fabric to wrap around the pipe and drainage rock or gravel, as shown.

2 **LAY THE PIPE** at the bottom of the trench, perforations down. Backfill the trench with about 4 inches of rock or gravel (be sure the pieces are bigger than the pipe perforations). Wrap the landscape fabric all the way around the pipe and gravel.

3 **FILL THE TRENCH** to the top with additional gravel or rock.

INSTALLING A CATCH BASIN. Ready-made catch basins are sold at building supply stores. Installing one is a relatively simple task. Follow these steps:

1 **DIG A HOLE** for the catch basin at the lowest point of the area that needs draining. Then dig a trench 8 inches deep and 8 inches wide for a solid-surface drainpipe, leading from the basin's side opening toward the disposal site.

2 **SET THE CATCH BASIN** into the hole you've dug, making sure its top is slightly below grade, and connect the pipe to the basin. Fill in with soil around the sides of the basin and in the trench, covering the pipe; set the basin's grate on top.

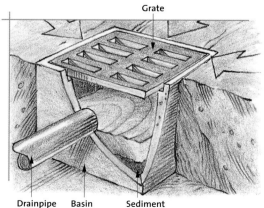

Grate

Drainpipe　　Basin　　Sediment

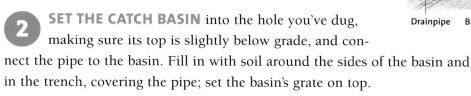

Drainage around Patios, Ponds, and Walls

All paved paths and patios should slope 1 inch every 8 feet so that water will drain off the surface away from the foundations of the house or any other structure. At the edge of the paving, you can install a French drain as shown at right. If paving abuts a bank, place a drain at that edge to prevent runoff from the bank from spilling onto the paving; slope your paving in that direction.

If the patio lies between the house and a retaining wall, slope the patio floor so that it drains like a bathtub, into a catch basin, as shown at right. Note the gravel backfill and drainpipe behind the retaining wall; weep holes built into the base of a wall are an alternate drainage option. Solid retaining walls may burst if water is allowed to dam up behind them. Dry-stacked walls are self-draining to some degree because water can seep through their joints, though added drainage makes them more stable.

A drain is necessary on the high side of a slope next to a pond. Otherwise the pressure of soil water behind the pond might pop a rigid pond out of its hole or warp and destabilize the pond edge. It's also important to keep runoff out of constructed streams and ponds to avoid flooding and blocked filters.

DRAINING PAVING AND SLOPES BEHIND WALLS

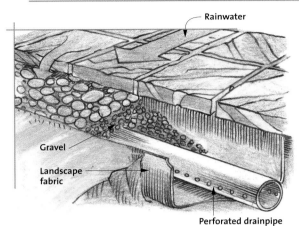

Rainwater

Gravel

Landscape fabric

Perforated drainpipe

Retaining wall

Drainpipe

Catch basin

DRAINING A POND BANK

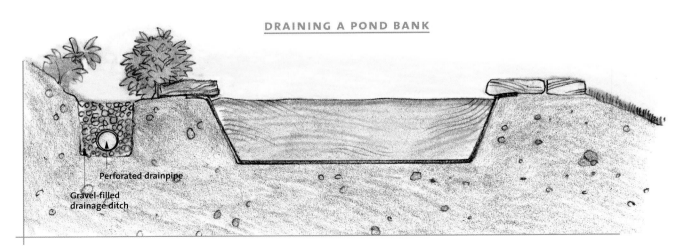

Perforated drainpipe

Gravel-filled drainage ditch

MEASURING YOUR SLOPE

MEASURING YOUR SLOPE PRODUCES INFORMATION YOU WILL USE IN SEVERAL WAYS. IT'S NECESSARY if your landscaping plan includes terraces or stairs. It can also tell you whether a lawn will be hard to mow, or whether there's an opportunity on a path to install a few steps.

Renting a surveyor's level, or transit, is the way to obtain exact measurements of elevation change on a long slope, but measurements good enough for most landscaping purposes can be made using either of the following simple methods. (For short distances, you need only a straight board, a carpenter's level, and a measuring tape—see page 88.)

Hillside gardens rarely slope in just one direction. Measure the grade change across the slope as well as from top to bottom.

Line-Level Method

A line level is a small, inexpensive level that hooks onto a string line. To measure a slope using a line level, first hammer a short stake into the ground at the top of the slope (A in the illustration below) and a tall stake into the ground at the bottom. The distance between the stakes should be no more than 50 feet.

Stretch and tie mason's line between the two stakes. Hang the level on the string and adjust the string until the bubble in the level is centered.

At the tall stake, use a tape to measure the distance from the string to the ground (B to C). This distance represents the drop-off, or vertical rise, in the slope between the top and bottom stakes. To figure out the grade, measure along the string line (from A to B) to get the horizontal run, then calculate as explained on page 76.

For a long slope, do the measuring in stages down the slope. Total the vertical distances for the drop-off and the horizontal measurements for the horizontal run.

MEASURING WITH A LINE LEVEL

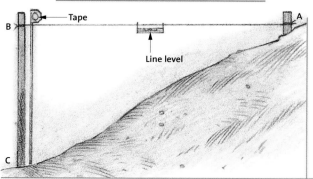

Tape

B

A

Line level

C

Hand-Level Method

A hand level is like a small telescope with a built-in level. It's good only for reading elevation change; it doesn't measure horizontal distances. (You'll need to measure the horizontal run with a line or tape.)

You'll need a helper and a measuring rod. You can make one by marking foot and inch increments on a 12-foot-long 1 by 2 or scrap piece of lumber. (If 12 feet isn't long enough for your slope, measure down the slope in increments and total all the drop-offs.) You could try using a wide steel tape instead of a lumber rod, but check to make sure it stays vertical—it might not on a windy day.

To determine your eye level in inches, have your helper hold the rod upright at a set reference point, such as the corner of the house. Standing erect nearby on a flat surface, look through the hand level at the rod until the bubble is centered. Read off the rod measurement intersected by the bubble and make a note of your eye-level measurement.

Now you can move to a position on the hillside and take a reading, standing erect, just as you did before. The distance on the rod above or below the eye-level measurement equals the difference in elevation: you simply subtract the eye-level measurement from your new reading. In the example in the illustrations, 63 inches (the eye-level measurement) is subtracted from 105 inches, giving a difference in elevation of 42 inches, or 3½ feet.

If your helper stays at the corner of the house with the rod, you can make a set of measurements from different places in your garden, pounding stakes into the ground at the various points and recording on them the elevations relative to the house.

Using a single reference point, such as the house, is ideal. If that's not possible, you can measure from several points, but be sure to key them to each other: list the initial reference point as zero and record in inches the elevation difference to the next reference point and any subsequent reference points. For simplicity, calculate all measurements relative to the initial reference point.

MEASURING WITH A HAND LEVEL

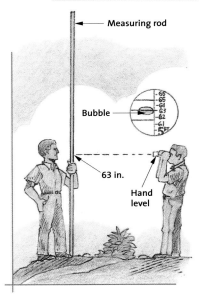

Measuring rod

Bubble

63 in.

Hand level

A hand level is good for determining elevation differences.

105 in.

GRADING

GRADING IS CALLED FOR IF YOUR PLAN INVOLVES LEVELING AREAS OR SMOOTHING OUT UNDULATING SLOPES. On hillsides that aren't too steep, it's fairly easy to do some kinds of recontouring—for example, creating a series of level planting beds or terraces (see page 80). You can probably muscle your way through a small job with a shovel and a wheelbarrow. If a lot of soil has to be shifted, though, you'll likely need to call in a professional with earth-moving equipment.

Study your hillside for clues as to how best to proceed. Calculate the grade in various areas and determine what you can do with the smallest amount of change. Rather than reshape your land, you may decide to work with what you have, simply planting the hillside and building circulation paths. Other than carving out a few steps here and there, that wouldn't require any real grading.

If you opt for extensive grading or major changes on a slope, consult a soils engineer, landscape architect, or other landscaping professional to ensure the stability of the hillside and to prevent drainage and erosion problems from occurring.

REMOVING TREES

Take care not to erode or destabilize your slope in the process of doing your landscaping. If you want to remove trees, leave their stumps and root systems in place to rot slowly instead of digging them out.

Calculating the Grade

The grade of a slope is its angle of steepness—how much it deviates from the horizontal. Usually this is expressed as a ratio or percentage. The ratio tells you how many feet of horizontal run there are for every foot of vertical rise. If, for example, the hillside rises 8 feet over the 40-foot distance from the house to the boundary fence, it has a slope ratio of 40:8, or 5:1.

Percentage of grade is the change in elevation over a distance of 100 feet. To calculate, divide the rise (8 feet, for example) by the run (say, 40 feet) and multiply by 100. In this case, the grade is 20 percent.

For instructions on how to measure elevation change and horizontal run, see the preceding two pages.

BELOW: This hillside has a slope ratio of 5:1, or a 20 percent grade.

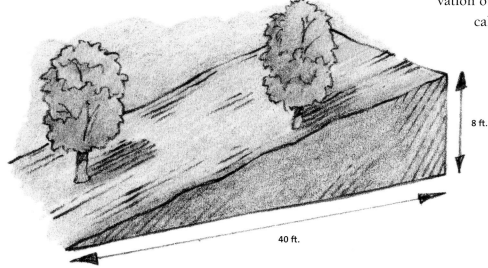

8 ft.

40 ft.

Types of Slope

Many hilly lots are graded when the land is developed for housing. The slope is cut to create a new grade and the excavated soil is used to fill another part of the original slope—as in the illustration below. This creates a level area for the house, patio, and lawn.

If your land was not graded, it may slope so irregularly that it could be described as undulating or rolling. If you despair at having such uneven terrain, consider that landscape architects go to great lengths to create a sense of topography on flat land. You may want to smooth out part of the slope to make planting or building easier, but it's often more interesting to work with the undulation; see Chapter 2 for ideas on the landscaping opportunities presented by natural topography.

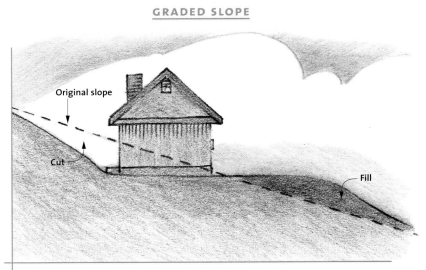

GRADED SLOPE

Original slope

Cut

Fill

Some part of your lot may slope gently enough that few allowances need be made for the grade—you may even be able to have a lawn on the slant without having a mowing problem. The grade doesn't have to become very steep, however, before turf becomes impractical, leaving alternatives such as ground covers. As the pitch increases, retaining walls, stairways, and decks are commonly incorporated to make land usable for gardening or outdoor living. Maximum and minimum grades for common landscape elements are shown in the chart below.

SUITABLE GRADES

Slope ratio	Percent grade	Angle (approx.)	
			Maximum for cut slopes
1:1	100%	45°	Maximum for fill slopes and ground covers
2:1	50%	27°	Maximum for simple construction
3:1	33%	18°	
4:1	25%	14°	Maximum for lawn—hard to mow
5:1	20%	12°	Maximum for lawn—easy to mow
10:1	10%	6°	Maximum for paths and ramps
20:1	5%	3°	Maximum for "flat" surface
100:1	1%	1°	Looks flat; minimum for drainage

THREE GRADING OPTIONS

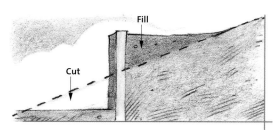

The slope is cut away and excess earth is moved downhill. The retaining wall now holds back a long terrace.

Soil is cut away and moved behind a tall retaining wall. The result is level ground below and a high terrace behind the wall.

Total wall height is divided between two terraces, resulting in a series of level beds.

Grading for a Retaining Wall

Locate a retaining wall so that it causes the least possible disruption of the natural slope. If space permits, the safest approach—and by far the easiest—is to build the wall on level ground near the foot of the slope and to fill in behind it. Other options (shown at left) disturb the hill and should be designed by an engineer unless walls are less than 3 feet tall (see pages 80–87). Note that in each of the situations shown here, the retaining wall rests on cut or undisturbed ground, not on fill. Never build on fill, which is prone to erosion and movement.

Whichever design you choose, plan to use the excavated soil as fill behind the retaining wall so that you won't have to import soil or have any hauled away.

Three Degrees of Slope

To a designer's eye, a slope in a garden is a blessing. It's an opportunity to introduce steps and walls, which not only provide visual interest and drama but also break up the space into two or more areas, making the garden seem larger. A number of design options are available for shallow and medium slopes, fewer for very steep slopes.

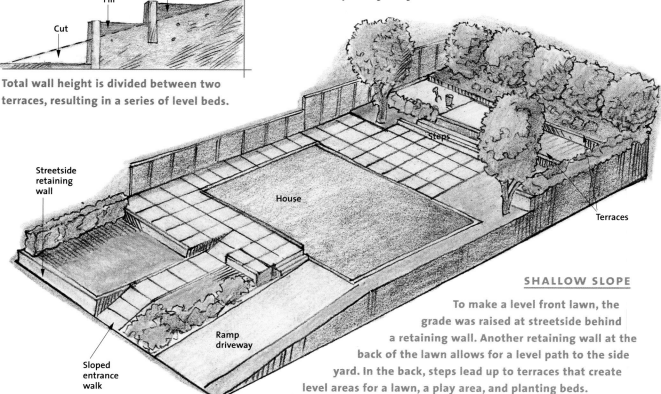

SHALLOW SLOPE

To make a level front lawn, the grade was raised at streetside behind a retaining wall. Another retaining wall at the back of the lawn allows for a level path to the side yard. In the back, steps lead up to terraces that create level areas for a lawn, a play area, and planting beds.

Streetside retaining wall

House

Steps

Terraces

Ramp driveway

Sloped entrance walk

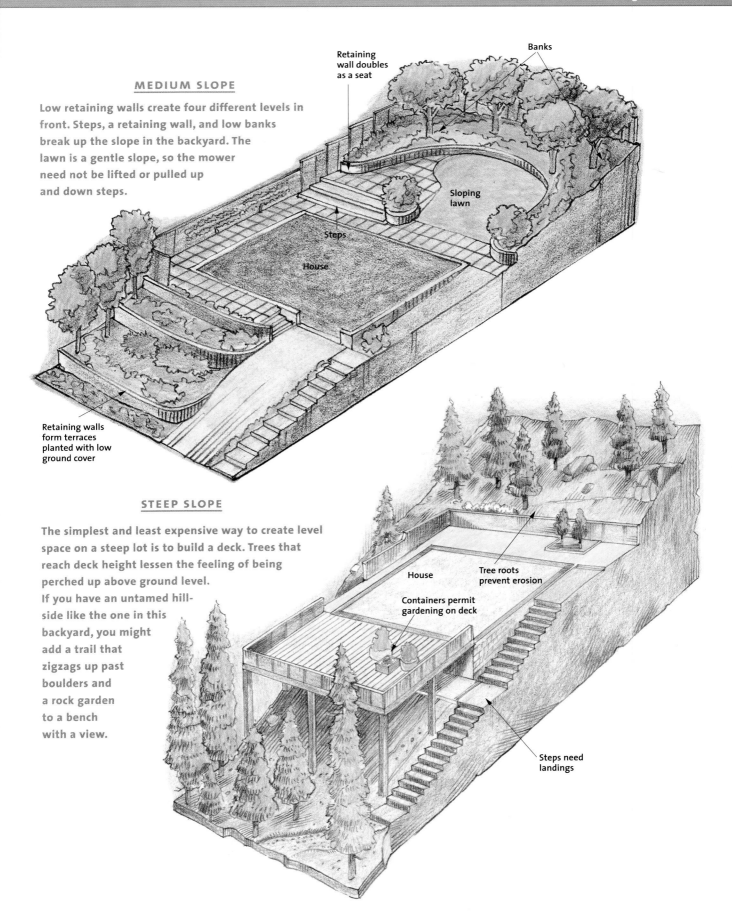

MEDIUM SLOPE

Low retaining walls create four different levels in front. Steps, a retaining wall, and low banks break up the slope in the backyard. The lawn is a gentle slope, so the mower need not be lifted or pulled up and down steps.

Retaining wall doubles as a seat

Banks

Sloping lawn

Steps

House

Retaining walls form terraces planted with low ground cover

STEEP SLOPE

The simplest and least expensive way to create level space on a steep lot is to build a deck. Trees that reach deck height lessen the feeling of being perched up above ground level. If you have an untamed hillside like the one in this backyard, you might add a trail that zigzags up past boulders and a rock garden to a bench with a view.

House

Tree roots prevent erosion

Containers permit gardening on deck

Steps need landings

TERRACES AND RETAINING WALLS

TERRACES AND THE WALLS THAT HOLD THEM IN PLACE CAN CURVE TO FOLLOW A HILLSIDE. ON MILD SLOPES, terraces may be large enough to accommodate lawns or ponds; on steeper hills, they tend to be narrow. Retaining walls range from hefty structures designed to hold back steep hillsides to low edgings for flower beds on slight slopes. They are different from freestanding garden walls in that they must be able to withstand the force of soil pushing against them.

OPEN TERRACES

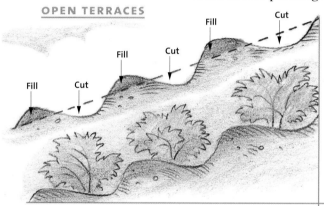

Fill

Cut

Fill

Cut

Fill

Cut

Fill

Cut

The Simplest Approaches

The simplest way to terrace a hillside is with a series of steps, as illustrated at left. You cut into the existing slope—perhaps as much as a foot, depending on how firm the soil is—and use the excavated soil to form a low berm at the front edge of each terrace. This gives you a level planting area and will slow the downhill flow of water, thus reducing erosion and allowing moisture to get to plant roots.

For a more permanent structure and wider planting areas, frame your terraces with retaining walls. See pages 34–37 for some ideas; any of the retaining-wall projects described in this section work well. In addition, check out the step-building projects on pages 88–93. Here we show two simple retaining constructions.

Riprap. An informal, natural-looking arrangement of stones, riprap is easy to build and needs no base. The stones are placed directly against an existing slope or bank in one layer or more. Basically a way to control erosion, riprap is suitable only for modest slopes. For stability, place the biggest stones at the base and partially bury the bottom layer. If you like, set plants in the spaces between rocks.

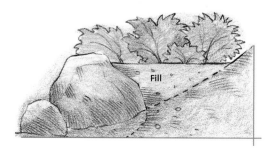

Fill

Boulder terrace. For a terraced planting that looks completely natural, position large rocks securely on a slope, fill in behind them with soil, and add plantings. Don't stack boulders; if you need more height, install a retaining wall as described on the following pages. For information on moving and installing boulders, see pages 132–133.

Choosing Retaining-Wall Material

Simple, low retaining walls on flat or gently sloping, stable ground are manageable do-it-yourself projects. The easiest materials to work with are modular concrete blocks, small rocks, railroad ties, and boards; projects using these materials are described on the following pages.

For a tall wall or where the ground is unstable or steep, you will need to call in a licensed engineer or landscape contractor. Building a steel-reinforced cast-concrete wall, the strongest type of retaining wall, is not a do-it-yourself job. A concrete-block wall is less expensive than a poured concrete one and nearly as strong, but again, unless you have building expertise, the project calls for hiring a contractor to build the block wall and reinforce it as necessary.

Brick is not a sound material for retaining walls much higher than 2 feet, even with steel reinforcing rods embedded in grout between double rows of brick. Most brick retaining walls built today—short as well as tall ones—actually consist of brick veneered onto, steel-reinforced concrete block.

A mortared stone wall is stronger than brick. You can build one up to about a foot tall on well-compacted soil. A taller wall requires a substantial concrete footing. You may want to hire a contractor to build the footing, then construct the actual wall yourself.

The owners' first thought was that they needed a single massive retaining wall, but by devising a series of small walls interspersed with planting beds, they created a terraced garden.

> **WORKING UP**
>
> When building tiers of terraces on a hillside, always start at the bottom of the slope and work your way upward.

Built-in Stability

Depending on the steepness of the slope and the height of the wall, the pressure pushing against a retaining wall can be tremendous, especially when heavy rains or melting snow saturate the hillside soil. It's important, therefore, even for a low retaining wall, to think about stability. Consider these points as you plan your wall:

- YOU MAY NEED A BUILDING PERMIT—check with your local building department. Many municipalities require permits for all retaining walls, while some have requirements only for structures over 3 feet high. You may be required to install a concrete foundation a certain depth below ground, especially where the ground freezes.
- LOCATE THE WALL on undisturbed or cut ground—never on fill, which is more prone to erosion and movement.
- IF YOU ARE BUILDING more than one retaining wall on a slope, start with the bottom one; doing it the other way around might undermine the wall you've just built.
- EVEN IF YOUR WALL doesn't require a footing, set the first layer of wall materials below grade.
- WHEN STACKING STONES or concrete modular blocks without mortar (a dry-laid wall—see pages 86–87), lean the face of the wall back into the slope to increase its stability; this lean is called the "batter," or cant. To achieve the right batter, build a batter gauge (see page 87).
- WHEN A RETAINING WALL FAILS poor drainage is often the cause. See page 73 for important information about providing adequate drainage behind a retaining wall.
- MAKE SURE THE SOIL or gravel behind your retaining wall is well compacted. Don't just shovel it in and tamp down the top. Add the fill in 6-inch layers and compact each layer thoroughly before adding more.

Modular Retaining Wall

To achieve something of the rustic look of a dry-stacked stone retaining wall without having to fit the stones carefully,

HOW TO FILL

Compact fill carefully—add soil in 6-inch layers and tamp it thoroughly before adding more.

A selection of thymes trails from the planting blocks in this modular retaining wall. For other planting ideas, see pages 152–155.

consider a modular wall built from interlocking concrete blocks. The pieces come in set sizes, and they interlock in such a way that the wall automatically steps back the correct amount from one layer, or "course," to the next.

Choose a style with a rough front face if you want the wall to resemble stone. If you want greenery to cover the wall eventually, choose blocks with hollow centers for soil and plants. All the modular systems allow you to turn corners and arrange the blocks in curves.

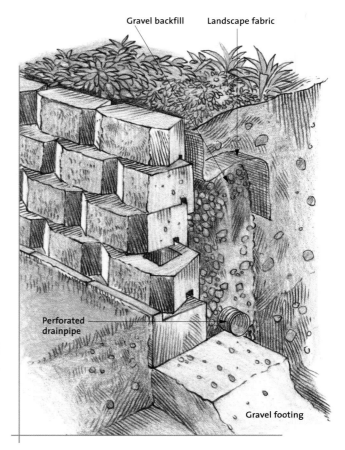

Gravel backfill   Landscape fabric

Perforated drainpipe

Gravel footing

1 **FOR A STRAIGHT WALL,** string mason's twine to mark the front edge. Dig a trench big enough for a 6-inch gravel layer under the first course and 6 to 8 inches of gravel behind the blocks (or whatever the manufacturer recommends). Compact the base with a hand tamper or, even better, a motorized plate compactor. Check that the base is level.

2 **LAY THE FOUNDATION ROW OF BLOCKS.** If the blocks have a rear lip, install the first row upside down and backward, as shown. To drain the area behind the wall, lay perforated drainpipe, hole side down, on the gravel. (See "Installing a French Drain," page 72.)

3 **LAY THE SECOND ROW,** staggering the joints over those of the first row. Backfill behind the wall with gravel, tamping it firm. Lay subsequent rows the same way, backfilling and compacting the gravel after laying each row.

4 **LAY CAPSTONES AT THE TOP OF THE WALL.** For systems that don't include capstones, manufacturers often recommend spreading a bead of construction adhesive on the top of the second-to-last row and firmly setting the top row onto that.

5 **SPREAD LANDSCAPE FABRIC** over the gravel backfill before you replace the topsoil behind the wall. The fabric will help prevent soil from clogging the gravel backfill and drainpipe.

Tie or Timber Retaining Wall

Top-quality railroad ties make good material for retaining walls, but if your choices are limited to ties that ooze creosote or are crooked or studded with nails, you may opt for a substitute—landscape timbers. These don't have the weathered charm of genuine ties, but they are more uniform. Railroad ties range from about 6 by 6 to 7 by 9 inches in thickness and 8 to 8½ feet in length. Timbers come in a wider range of sizes.

To provide drainage, excavate into the slope so that you can install gravel behind the wall and lay perforated drainpipe on the gravel (see "Installing a French Drain," page 72).

Ties or timbers are usually laid horizontally. To begin, partially bury the first course of wood. For added strength, set each additional course back about an inch and stagger the joints. Anchor the wall to the ground by drilling holes about 4 feet apart through all the layers, then pounding galvanized steel pipe or reinforcing bar into the holes. Use rods long enough that there's at least as much steel in the ground as above it.

As an alternative, you can set ties or timbers vertically. Cut them long enough that about two-thirds of their length will be in the ground. To strengthen the wall, set the ends in concrete and fasten building paper to the back side of the wall.

TIES OR TIMBERS LAID HORIZONTALLY

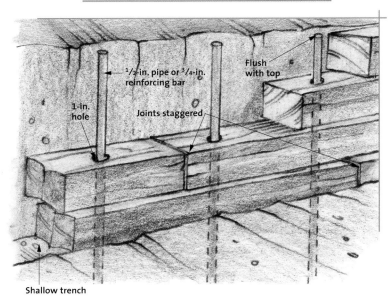

½-in. pipe or ¾-in. reinforcing bar

Flush with top

1-in. hole

Joints staggered

Shallow trench

TIES OR TIMBERS LAID VERTICALLY

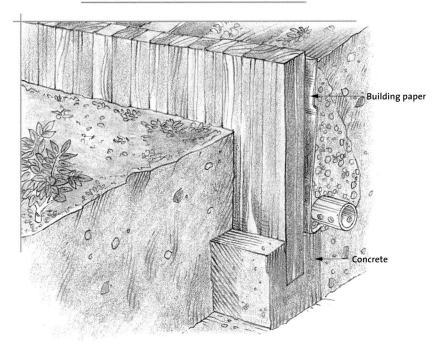

Building paper

Concrete

Board Retaining Wall

For a board wall, attach wide boards to 4-by-4 posts. The posts should be twice the height of the finished wall, since half their length will be buried. Position the posts no more than 4 feet apart; see page 96 for guidelines on setting them. When attaching the boards, stagger the joints so they don't all line up at the same posts.

For visible posts, nail or screw on the boards on the upslope side of the wall. For hidden posts, attach boards to the front side with carriage bolts, which have attractive rounded heads. Use two bolts per board at each splice and two on boards that span a post. Line the back with moisture-proof building paper to extend the wall's life by several years.

To drain the area behind the wall, excavate into the slope and install gravel before you start building. Lay perforated drainpipe on the gravel, hole side down, sloped downhill to where you want the water to drain out (see "Installing a French Drain," page 72).

ABOVE: A board retaining wall blends well with a built-in wooden seat and arbor amid lush plantings.

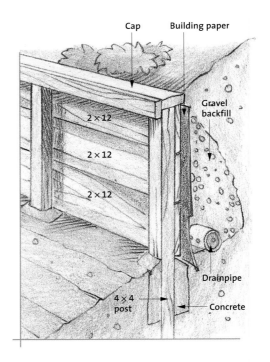

A sphere makes a decorative insert in a stone wall.

Dry-Laid Stone Retaining Wall

Large, stackable stones or broken concrete pieces can be laid in courses without mortar; their weight holds them in place. Laid dry, a stone wall doesn't need a concrete footing if it's kept fairly low (to about 3 feet tall). Instead, the foundation can be a 4- to 6-inch-thick base of well-compacted angular gravel, crushed stone, road base, or coarse sand. Don't use pea gravel or other rounded gravel for the pad or backfill—these materials don't compress well.

To drain the area behind a dry-stacked wall, excavate into the slope so that you can install gravel. Lay perforated drainpipe on the gravel, hole side down (see "Installing a French Drain," page 72).

1 **DIG A 2-FOOT-WIDE TRENCH** deep enough to accommodate the base and a partially buried first course of stone. Use a carpenter's level to check that the foundation is even. If the length of the wall is on sloping terrain, create a stepped foundation and start building the wall at the lowest elevation.

2 **LAY THE FOUNDATION STONES,** placing a large, long base stone across each end of the trench. Choose well-shaped stones for the face of the wall, the largest on the bottom; work from the outsides in, and pack the smallest stones in the center of the wall.

3 **LAY THE SECOND COURSE,** staggering joints so that a full stone sits above the juncture of two stones—"one stone over two, two over one" is the stonemason's rule. Place bond stones (long stones that span the wall's width, like the base stones) every few feet to tie the wall together. Step each course back slightly so that the wall leans into the slope; a batter of about 2 inches per foot of rise is good. Gently tap small stones into gaps with a mason's hammer, being careful not to dislodge stones you've already set.

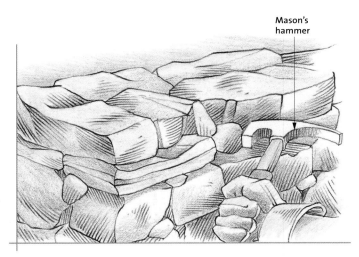

Mason's hammer

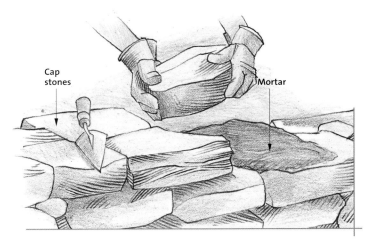

Cap stones

Mortar

4 **FINISH THE TOP** with as many flat, broad cap stones as possible. If you live in an area that experiences frost, mortar the cap stones. This will allow water to drain off and help prevent ice from forming between stones and pushing them apart.

Making a Batter Gauge

To take the guesswork out of calculating your wall's batter, or tilt, make a gauge from 1-by-2 wood strips. Nail together at a right angle a vertical piece equal to the wall height and a horizontal piece equal to the batter at the top of the wall—2 inches per foot of height. (For example, the batter for a 3-foot-tall wall would be 6 inches.) Nail a third strip to the ends of the other two to form a triangle, making sure the first two pieces stay at a right angle. To check batter as you build , hold the vertical strip plumb against a level, as shown at right.

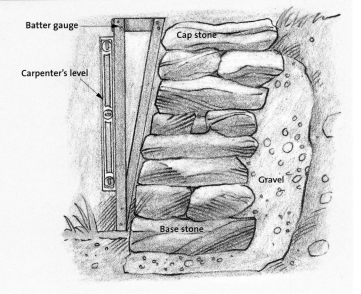

Batter gauge

Cap stone

Carpenter's level

Gravel

Base stone

STEPS

WHEN SLOPES HAVE A GRADE OF AT LEAST **10** PERCENT (a rise or fall of 1 foot for every 10 feet of distance), steps are necessary for comfortable walking. They aren't usually needed on gentler grades, although you may want some for surer footing or design purposes. Choose a material that complements your garden's style but doesn't compromise safety; the steps should not pose a hazard in wet weather.

Figuring the Proportions

The reason some steps are pleasant to climb while others seem a nuisance could simply be their proportions. This handy formula sums up what tends to work in terms of a comfortable stride: the depth of the tread plus twice the rise should equal 25 to 27 inches (see chart at left). All risers need to be the same height, for safety.

For outdoor steps, a rise of 4 to 6$\frac{1}{2}$ inches ensures an easy climb; between 5 and 7 inches gets people up and down quickly but still safely. Stair treads should be at least 13 inches deep. The ideal combination is a 15-inch tread with a 6-inch rise.

Fitting Steps to a Slope

Begin designing your steps by measuring the slope. If you are creating a long flight of steps, use the methods described on pages 74–75. For a short distance, enlist a helper and extend a long, straight board horizontally from the top of the slope, as shown below left. When the board is level, measure its height from the bottom of the slope. This is the "rise." The "run" is the horizontal distance back to the top of the slope.

To determine the number and dimensions of steps you need, decide first what riser height you'd like. Divide that into the total rise (in inches). Round off the fraction to the closest whole number and you'll have the number of steps you need. Divide the run by the number of steps, and you'll have the tread measurement.

Compare your rise and tread figures to the chart and the formula described above. Rarely will the numbers work out the first time. Try adjusting the riser height. If your slope is too steep even for 7-inch risers, remember that steps don't need to attack a slope head-on: an attractive solution is an L-shaped series of steps, or even a U-shaped series (across the slope, not too steeply, then straight up for a short stint, and then back across the slope).

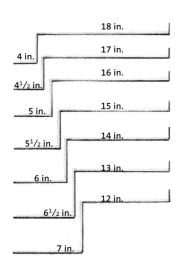

STEP PROPORTIONS

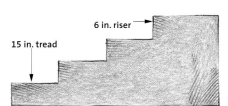

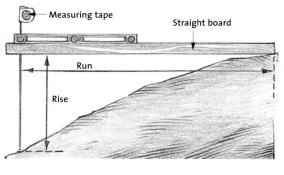

MEASURING RISE AND RUN

Ramp Steps

On gentle to moderate slopes, one option is ramp steps—a succession of single steps with long ramps between them. Make the ramp length uniform—for example, 6, 8, or 10 feet—so that people can anticipate the next step as they walk.

Landscape timbers form the front of these ramp steps. Galvanized pipe or rebar pins timbers to the ground (see page 91).

Step Safety

Don't compromise safety to get the rise and tread measurements that you want. As you fine-tune the layout of your steps, here are some safety pointers to keep in mind:

• The closer steps come to allowing a normal walking stride, the safer they are to climb; the chart on the facing page shows good proportions. Don't make steps lower than 4 inches—you'll find yourself taking two at a time, which can be dangerous, particularly if your hands are full.

• To give people a place to catch their breath on long flights of stairs and to break a fall if anyone slips, divide flights of more than five steps into sections separated by a landing at least 4 feet long.

• Avoid using just one step along a path—people won't expect it and may trip. Fit in a second step or eliminate steps altogether and curve a sloping path up the hillside instead.

• Consider whether you need lighting along the steps. If you build a retaining wall to bolster your stairs, you can incorporate light fixtures into it. Fixtures should cast light on the treads but not into people's eyes.

Yellow-flowered money-wort *(Lysimachia)* has spread from the garden across these stepping-stone steps. Many rock garden plants also grow well between steps (see pages 152–155).

Construction Pointers

Before you begin building your steps, there are a few important construction factors to take into consideration.

● MAKE THE STEPS at least as wide as the path. They may be much broader if you want to incorporate seating or pots of plants.

● FOR DRAINAGE, slope the surface of each tread 1 to 2 percent (about $\frac{1}{8}$ to $\frac{1}{4}$ inch per foot) down toward its riser, or slope it sideways to run water into a channel at the edge of the steps.

● PLAN HOW you'll keep dirt from washing down the slope onto your steps. Two options are burying stones halfway at both sides of the steps or building a small wall alongside the stairs.

● YOUR CALCULATIONS of riser height need to be precise before you start building—you can't fudge with the height once you begin. The calculation method described on page 88 assumes the bottom step is at ground level and the paving or landing stone at the top of the stairway matches the thickness of the treads. Make any adjustments before you begin.

Stepping-Stone Steps

If you need just a few steps and have a way to get big, heavy stones to your site, you can build a stepping-stone staircase. Use irregularly shaped flagstone or large blocks of cut stone, each at least 20 inches long, 24 inches wide, and about 6 inches thick. Each stone will make one step. Buy one extra piece to serve as a foundation stone.

Tilt forward or to side by $\frac{1}{8}$ in. per foot

Sand

Mortar (optional)

1 STARTING AT THE BOTTOM of the slope, dig a foundation hole that's as big around as the stone. Make it as deep as the stone if you live where winters are mild. If you live where the ground freezes, excavate 4 to 6 inches deeper and pack that space with crushed gravel.

2 ADD SAND and pack it into a 2-inch layer with a hand tamper, or mist the sand to settle it thoroughly. Wait for any puddles to drain.

3 MOVE THE FIRST STONE onto the damp sand, twisting or tamping it until it is just slightly sloped and about 2 inches above the surrounding soil. If there is a gap behind the stone, pack it with soil or gravel.

4 **DIG BACK BEHIND THE FOUNDATION STONE** to create enough room for the second stone, plus about an inch of sand (use more sand if stones are bumpy). Place the next step so that it overlaps the foundation stone by at least 1 inch. To level the step, twist it into the sand or shim under the front with thin, flat stones. Fill around the shims with mortar if you wish, but don't expect mortar to glue wobbly stones together.

5 **INSTALL THE REST OF THE STONES THE SAME WAY.** When all the steps are in place, dig back some of the bank alongside the steps and embed large stones there to keep soil from washing down the steps.

Steps of Ties or Timbers

Railroad ties or pressure-treated landscape timbers make simple, rugged risers that can be teamed with gravel or another tread material. Many railroad ties are 8 feet long and can be cut in half for 4-foot-wide steps, although their widths, which become the stair risers, may vary somewhat. Landscape timbers come in a range of lengths and more uniform widths (choose 6 by 6s or larger; 4 by 4s are too small to make comfortable steps).

For the most stable steps, make a box frame for each tread, as described here. (You can also use timbers for just the front edge of each step, as a simple riser, and edge the steps with field-stone; see the photograph on page 89.)

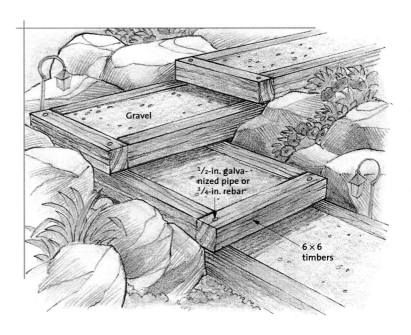

Gravel

$\frac{1}{2}$-in. galvanized pipe or $\frac{3}{4}$-in. rebar

6 × 6 timbers

1 **LEVEL AN AREA FOR THE BOTTOM STEP.** Build the timber frame in place, making sure it's level. Drill holes in the front two corners and drive 18-inch-long pieces of $\frac{1}{2}$-inch galvanized pipe or $\frac{3}{4}$-inch rebar through the wood to pin it to the ground. Pound the metal a little below the top of the wood.

2 **EXCAVATE ABOVE AND BEHIND** the first step to create a level place for the second one. Build the second frame so that its front piece rests on the back of the first frame. Drill through the overlapped corners and pound pipe or rebar through the holes into the soil. Continue in this way up the slope.

3 **FILL THE FRAMES** with crushed gravel, such as $\frac{5}{8}$-inch with smaller particles included, and pack it in well.

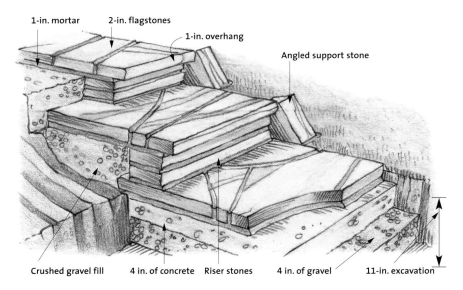

1-in. mortar 2-in. flagstones 1-in. overhang Angled support stone

Crushed gravel fill 4 in. of concrete Riser stones 4 in. of gravel 11-in. excavation

Flagstone Steps

Building a flight of flagstone steps is a significant project; you may want to have it done by a professional. Be sure that the steps rest on undisturbed soil.

Create treads from 2-inch-thick flagstones, either single slabs or small pieces mortared together. For risers, use either granite cobblestones, 4 or 5 inches thick, or one or two layers of ledgestone (stone trimmed to uniformly thick, rectangular pieces). You will also need two rectangular cobblestones for support pieces for each step; $5/8$-inch crushed gravel with smaller particles included; concrete; and mortar.

To prepare, place the flagstones in tread-size arrangements. Each tread should be big enough that you can place the granite riser blocks for the next step on its back edge and still leave the tread depth you want. Cut the stones as necessary so pieces fit nicely, separated by about $1/2$ inch.

1 MEASURE along the level board or string that you used to calculate the dimensions of your steps and mark the beginning and end of each tread. Transfer these marks to the ground with a plumb bob on a string; drive a stake into each spot. Use a carpenter's square to establish the two sides of the steps. Drive stakes at those corners, too.

2 EXCAVATE the rough shape of the steps.

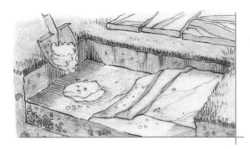

3 ARRANGE THE STONES for the bottom tread, which will be flush with the soil. Mark the outline, remove the stones, and dig down 11 inches. Pack the excavation with 4 inches of gravel.

Prepare bagged concrete mix. Shovel it over the gravel, making a 4-inch layer. Smooth the surface (it doesn't need to be perfect) and wait at least 24 hours.

4 AT EACH SIDE, dig out enough soil so you can place one rectangular cobblestone at a 45-degree angle, far enough forward to protrude in front of the riser stones.

Prepare mortar (if homemade, mix 1 part masonry cement to 3 parts masonry sand). Add just enough water for a stiff mixture. Spread a 1-inch layer on the concrete and a 2-inch layer around the edge cobblestones. Place the tread flagstones, jiggling them slightly to set them. With a rubber mallet, tap them level or tipped very slightly toward the front.

With a trowel, fill the spaces between stones with mortar. When it stiffens slightly, stuff it down with the trowel. Cut away excess mortar and lift it off. Clean up residue with a damp sponge. Cover the step with plastic for at least 24 hours and keep off the paving for three days.

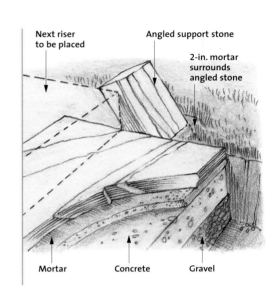

Next riser to be placed · Angled support stone · 2-in. mortar surrounds angled stone · Mortar · Concrete · Gravel

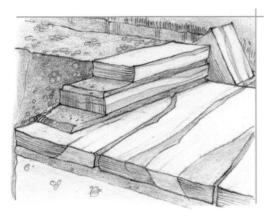

5 TO BUILD THE NEXT STEP, spread a 1-inch mortar layer as wide as the riser stones over the back edge of the flagstones. Position the riser stones on top, filling between them with mortar. Level the stones and wipe away smears.

After the mortar sets (cover the riser with plastic and wait at least 24 hours), carefully dig a 6-inch-deep hole behind the risers big enough to accommodate the next tread. Add 3 inches of gravel, tamp, add more gravel, and pack it down firmly; the stability of the steps depends on well-compacted gravel. Continue until the gravel is level with the top of the riser stones. Mix more mortar and spread a 1-inch layer over the crushed gravel and the riser stones. Set the tread flagstones in place, with 1 inch overhanging the riser. Tap the stones level.

Repeat until you have installed the final step.

THE LAST RISER

If you see that your riser spacing is off as you reach the top step, don't attempt to alter the riser height. Adjust the soil level at the top of the slope to accommodate the last step.

FENCES AND GATES

A HILLSIDE POSES NO BARRIER TO BUILDING A FENCE, ALTHOUGH YOU'LL HAVE TO CONSTRUCT IT DIFFERENTLY than you would on level ground. A fence may follow the slope's natural contours or step down the hillside in a series of level sections. A gate can also work on a slope if you give a little thought to the hinges and swing direction.

CONTOURED POST-AND-RAIL FENCE

STEPPED POST-AND-RAIL FENCE

STEPPED BOARD FENCE

Contoured or Stepped?

A contoured fence runs parallel to the slope of a hillside, while a stepped fence is laid out in level sections like stair steps. The easier of the two to build, a contoured fence works on almost any slope, even along bumpy terrain. But you may prefer the appearance of a stepped fence, especially as viewed in relationship to the house. A contoured fence tends to look lopsided against straight architectural lines.

For contoured fencing, consider building a post-and-rail fence or a solid fence of pickets, palings, or grape stakes. For stepped fencing, common choices include board, louver, basket-weave, and panel construction. See pages 52–53 for ideas, and choose a design that complements your house and garden. If you decide on panel fencing, it needs to be tall enough that you can cut the bottom of the fence to follow the contour of the slope; otherwise you'll end up with triangular gaps at the bottom.

Planning Ahead

Before you set the first post or decide on fence height, check with your local building department about any required setbacks or restrictions on height and material. For example, there may be a rule dictating that the "good side" of the fence (the side to which the siding is affixed) face the neighboring property.

If your fence is to run along a bank or cliff, it's a good idea to consult a landscape architect or engineer; the site may require a retaining wall or deep anchoring posts. Hiring a professional also makes sense for laying out a fence across very steep or irregularly sloped land.

For lumber fences, be sure to choose decay-resistant (redwood, cedar, or cypress) or pressure-treated wood.

When you are ready to start construction, ask a friend to help so that the work goes more easily.

Plotting a Fence

The first step in building a fence is to mark the exact path it will take and where the posts will go. Drive in the end stakes and stretch mason's line between them. Tie the line to the stakes at a set distance off the ground, high enough to clear the ground and any plantings. For uneven terrain, you may need to tie the line to intermediate stakes.

To determine how many posts you'll need, measure the distance along the string in feet; using a maximum post spacing of 8 feet, divide the total  fence distance by 8. If the resulting number ends in a fraction, round up to the next whole number. Divide the total distance by that number to get the exact spacing between posts (the distance between the center of one post to the center of the next post).

Measure and mark the post locations on the string. Then dangle a plumb bob to transfer the marks you made on the string to the ground beneath—for example, by driving nails through pieces of paper into the soil.

If you are plotting a stepped fence, you'll need to calculate how much to step down each section, post to post. Follow the instructions on pages 74–75 for measuring the elevation change along the fence line. Convert that to inches and divide by the number of fence sections. For example, a 30-inch height differential along a fence line divided into four sections results in a $7\frac{1}{2}$-inch drop per section.

See the following page for instructions on building a board fence.

Board Fences

Generally, posts for board fences are 4 by 4s and rails are 2 by 4s. You have various siding options, such as grape stakes, elegant pickets, and clapboard.

For fences 3 to 6 feet tall, plan to set posts in concrete at least 2 feet deep, a foot deeper for the end and gate posts. For taller fences, the rule of thumb for post depth is a third of the post length. To get the post tops even, either dig postholes to an exact uniform depth or cut the posts after they are installed. To make the job of digging the holes easier, use a post-hole digger or rent a power auger.

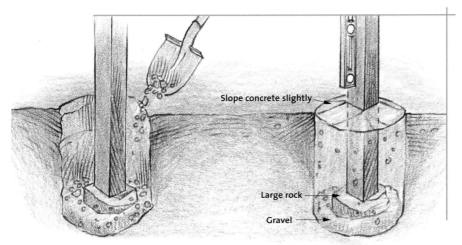

Slope concrete slightly

Large rock

Gravel

1 **DIG THE HOLES** 6 inches deeper than the recommended post depth and three times the post diameter. Place a rock at the base of each hole and add 6 inches of gravel.

Starting at one end, center the post in the hole and shovel in concrete, tamping it down with a broomstick or capped pipe to remove air pockets. Use a level to check that the post is plumb. Fill to 1 to 2 inches above ground level, sloping the concrete away from the post to divert water. Brace the post with 1-by-4 stakes while the concrete cures.

Repeat for the other end post. Make sure the faces of the two posts are parallel and plumb. After setting a post in concrete, you have about 20 minutes to align it to the other posts before the concrete hardens.

2 **INSTALL THE LINE POSTS.** To make it easier to align them, tack 1-by-2 spacer blocks to the end posts, string mason's line between them, and set each post a block's thickness from the line. Fill and level the concrete as described in Step 1. Let cure for two days. Remove the blocks. If necessary, cut posts to height.

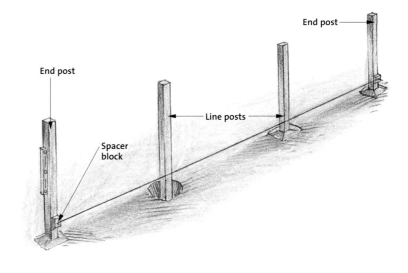

End post

End post

Line posts

Spacer block

3 **ATTACH RAILS.** You can butt them against the post and toenail them (nailing at an angle into the post), notch them in (cut notches before installing posts), or lap them over the sides or top of each post. You can also use metal brackets. Brush on wood preservative where rails and posts will meet. Then fasten one end of each rail, enlist a helper to check the level, and secure the other end.

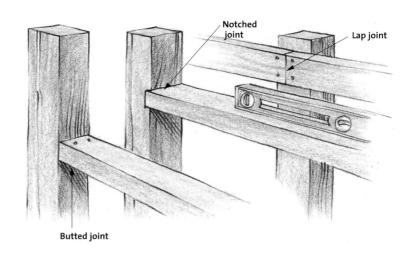

Notched joint

Lap joint

Butted joint

4 **CUT THE SIDING BOARDS.** Check the first board for plumb and then secure it to the rails with screws roughly three times as long as the board's thickness. Secure additional boards, one by one, cutting the bottom ends on the slant to follow the slope. Check the alignment of each board as you go.

Designing a Gate

Make gates at least 3 feet wide (4 feet is better) to accommodate a wheelbarrow or garden cart. You can cut the siding at the bottom of the gate to follow the slope if you hinge the gate on the downhill side (it can swing in either direction). A gate that is perpendicular to the slope—across the slope, as shown in the foreground here, rather than parallel to it—must be hinged to swing downhill. A gate installed on level ground (as shown in the background) can be hinged on either side. Be sure to allow adequate clearance for sturdy hinges.

PATHS

PATHS DIRECT VISITORS AROUND THE GARDEN AND PRO-VIDE ACCESS TO THE PLACES YOU MOST WANT THEM TO SEE. Paths near the house are usually constructed of the most elegant materials; the closer to the end of the garden they go, the more rustic paths tend to be. See pages 26–29 for design ideas. Then plan and build your paths using the information presented here.

Planning a Path

There's no better way to decide on the course of a path than by walking up and down and across your garden to experience for yourself just how comfortable it is to ascend a certain grade, or where you might like a bend in the path or a small landing. The main path should take you to views and offer several places to sit or pause, but you'll probably need small paths into the backs of flower beds and shrub borders, too, so you can tend the plantings there. All your paths should be comfortable for their purpose.

BELOW: Incorporating steps is the most direct way to take a path uphill, but curving or zigzagging the path may make for a gentler ascent.

REDUCING THE STEEPNESS OF THE CLIMB

To decrease the steepness of a path, meander or zigzag it across the slope. It's quite comfortable for most people to walk on a path that slopes up to 5 percent (6 inches of rise or fall for every 10 feet of distance), but the grade can be as steep as 10 percent before steps are necessary.

An entrance pathway should be at least 4 feet wide; 6 feet allows two people to walk abreast. For an informal garden path, 3 feet is the usual width. Be sure a path can accommodate a wheelbarrow or other equipment that will be conveyed along it.

To mark your proposed pathway, insert stakes or spray water-soluble paint. As you plan the path, decide how you will edge it, if necessary; install the edging before laying the path materials.

Simplest and Not So Simple

Although you'll need to replenish it every year or two, a mulch path (bottom) is the least expensive and easiest type to install. Just spread the mulch (in this case, macadamia nut husks) on the soil surface—there's no need to trench or install edgings.

Poured concrete (right) makes a stable walking surface on gently sloping terrain, especially if it is textured or pattern-stamped to provide traction in wet weather. It can also be tinted to add interest and soften the look of the walkway. But installing a concrete path may be complicated and costly, depending on how much you can do yourself. Unless you've had construction experience, you'll want to call in a qualified professional to construct the forms, pour the concrete, and finish the surface.

Concrete Stones

If you like the idea of cast concrete stepping-stones, you can cast your own, as designer Harland Hand did here. For each stone, mark out a large elliptical area on the soil, at least 2 feet wide. Shovel ready-mix concrete onto

the area. Use a trowel to tamp and smooth it into a stone about 3 inches thick, tapering at the edges so the stone seems to rise up from bedrock. Before the concrete is dry, mix a color tint with some dry cement and smear and trowel it into the surface. Leave the surface a little rough, for traction. Keep the stones damp for several days to cure the concrete.

Stepping-Stone Paths

You can lay stepping-stones to follow gently rolling terrain. Where they cross grass, set them a little below grade so the mower can pass over them easily, and where they cross wet areas, set them high. Overlap the stones in steep places to make simple steps (see page 90), and lay a group of them on flat areas to form a simple landing.

Shopping for stepping-stones. Choose a thick, heavy material, such as large flagstone pieces, broken concrete, or cast concrete. Thin or small pieces of stone are unlikely to stay put on a slope, especially following frosts and heavy rains. The most natural-looking stepping-stones have rough, pocked surfaces, which are good for traction, but avoid stones with indentations in the center—if water collects there and freezes, the path will become dangerous.

Measure the length of your path before you shop for stones. If each stone will be about 18 inches front to back (a comfortable size for stepping onto) and you've decided on 6-inch gaps between stones (see Step 1, below), you'll need one stone for every 2 feet of path. It doesn't matter how wide the stones are—20 inches or even 36 inches—because you'll lay the long side across the path. For a small project, it's worth spending time matching stone shapes; see page 29.

Laying stepping-stones. Stepping-stones are generally set 1 or 2 inches above the surrounding soil so the path stays free of mud. You can set them directly on soil, but a sand base makes it easier to keep them from wobbling, important for safety. If an area is particularly damp or if you live where spring thaws tend to buckle the soil surface, install 4 to 8 inches of gravel beneath the stones to help ensure good drainage.

1 **PLACE STONES** so their longest dimension runs across the path, not in line with it. Decide on spacing: 10 to 12 inches between stones encourages a fast pace, suitable for a functional path; 4 inches slows people down, invites them to linger.

2 **CUT AROUND THE FIRST STONE** with a spade or knife to mark its shape. Then tip the stone on edge and roll it to the side.

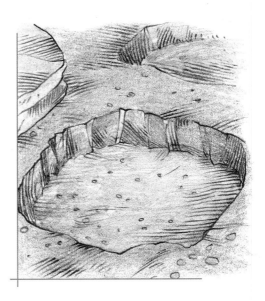

3 **EXCAVATE A HOLE** half as deep as the stone is thick (so it will be embedded) plus 1 inch for a sand base. (A stone 4 inches thick needs a hole at least 3 inches deep.) Cut the edges straight down with a straight-edged spade. Remove the soil within the outline.

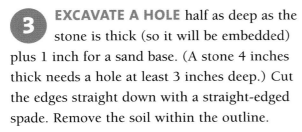

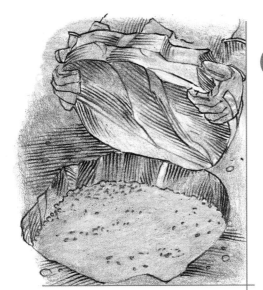

4 **SPREAD 1 INCH OF SAND** in the hole. Dampen with a fine spray of water. Tip the stone back into place, twisting it into the sand until it is level and firm.

5 **ADD MORE SAND** around the stone and pack the edges. Water with a fine spray to settle the sand.

Repeat these steps for all the remaining stones.

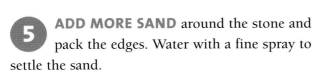

Aubrieta and other drought-tolerant rock-garden plants grow well in gravel that isn't packed too hard or deep. Recommended plants for rocky ground are described on pages 152–155.

Gravel Paths

A gravel path is inexpensive and easy to build. It never becomes slippery, and rainwater will tend to seep through it into the soil, a good thing on a hillside (water sheeting off a solid path surface can cause erosion). The steeper the path, the more likely it is that the gravel will gradually move downhill, so edge the path firmly and expect to spread additional gravel periodically.

Shopping for gravel. Gravel comes in many colors, different sizes, and either round or crushed. If you want a path that crunches and is loose underfoot, buy natural or beach gravel, also known as pea gravel, for the surface material. Gravel of this type consists of rounded stones that are all one size. Diameters of $\frac{3}{8}$, $\frac{1}{2}$, or $\frac{5}{8}$ inch work well.

For a quiet path, get crushed gravel that includes fine particles. The sharp edges of the gravel interlock and the small particles fill spaces, creating a firm mass that is more likely than loose gravel to stay put on a slope. Specify the maximum size of gravel and then add "minus" to your request to indicate that you want smaller particles included. A $\frac{5}{8}$-minus mix, for example, consists of pieces ranging down from $\frac{5}{8}$ inch in diameter. For a smoother surface, choose smaller gravels. Both $\frac{1}{4}$-minus gravel and decomposed granite, a very fine by-product of granite mining, pack down to look and feel almost like pavement; either is an excellent choice if you will be running wheelbarrows, bicycles, or carts along the path.

To calculate quantities, decide on the depth (usually 3 to 6 inches; see facing page). Convert all measurements to feet. Multiply the width by the length of the path, then multiply the result by the depth. Divide the resulting number by 27 and you will have the cubic yards needed. Consider ordering 5 to 10 percent extra to be sure you don't run short.

Landscape Fabric: Yes or No?

Some gardeners spread landscape fabric, also known as weed cloth, beneath gravel or mulch paths. But it is no panacea. While it blocks sprouts and runners from coming up from below, it doesn't prevent seeds that land on the surface from sprouting (and sometimes growing down into the cloth, where they're harder to remove).

Prevent weed growth just as effectively by keeping the path clean of decaying leaves and soil so that weed seedlings have little chance to survive. Pull weeds that do sprout while they're still small.

Layering path materials. If you are using crushed gravel, you can fill the entire excavation with it. But sometimes it makes sense to have two or three layers of different types of materials.

● IF YOU SELECT A TYPE OF GRAVEL that's particularly expensive, save money by using it only for the top couple of inches and use less expensive gravel or sand underneath.

● **IF YOU ARE WORRIED ABOUT DRAINAGE,** fill the bottom of the excavation with 3 inches of ³⁄₄-inch gravel. Cover that with landscape fabric and then put sand or smaller gravel with "fines" (a minus mix) on top.

● **IF YOU WANT ROUND PEBBLES** on the surface, use crushed gravel or sand on the bottom and add only a couple of inches of the round pebbles. Otherwise, the path will be hard to walk on.

Making a gravel path. The following instructions are for a basic 3-inch-deep gravel path. Installing a deeper base (3 inches or more of gravel instead of just 1 inch) will make a path that's sturdier, easier to maintain, and better draining.

1 **EXCAVATE THE PATH AREA** to a depth of at least 3 inches. Install the edging first. In the illustration, fieldstones form the path boundary; see pages 104–105 for other options. If you are using landscape fabric (see facing page), install it now. Add a 1-inch base of sand or crushed gravel.

2 **RAKE THE SAND** or crushed gravel to a uniform thickness, then dampen it with a fine spray of water.

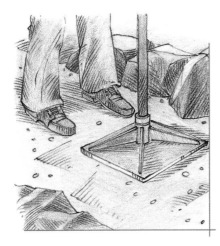

3 **PASS OVER THE AREA** several times with a hand tamper to pack the base firmly. If you have a long, straight path, you can use a motorized plate compactor instead, but switch to a hand tamper along the edges.

4 **ADD SURFACE GRAVEL MATERIAL** (see "Shopping for Gravel," facing page), at least 2 inches thick. Rake it evenly over the base and tamp it firmly in place.

PLASTIC EDGING

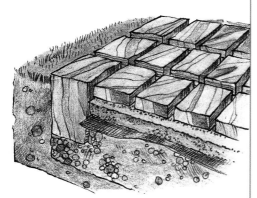

CUT-STONE EDGING

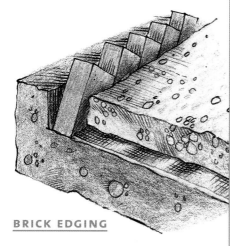

BRICK EDGING

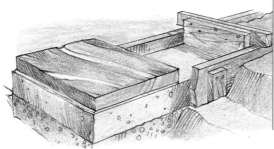

CONCRETE EDGING

Path Edgings

Edgings act as a physical barrier to prevent a piece of stone or brick from slipping at the path edge or to keep gravel from mixing with the surrounding soil. They also lock in place the setting bed, the layer of sand or gravel beneath the surface material. If that base isn't stable, the surface material will sink or warp, bricks and stone may crack, and path maintenance will be altogether higher.

Choosing an edging. Some edgings are barely noticeable, while others are decorative, designed to complement and contribute to the style of a path.

- WOOD OR COMPOSITES of plastic and wood fiber are a popular choice. Wood should be either naturally rot-resistant (such as the dark-colored heartwood of cedar or redwood) or pressure-treated with preservatives. See the facing page for installation instructions.

- PLASTIC EDGING is available at masonry-supply stores and home centers in several styles. For gravel paths, get rolls with a wide, rounded top edge. For stone paving at least $1^{1}/_{2}$ inches thick, look for the type designed for brick paving (shown at top left). Metal strip edging is also available in some stores; like plastic edging, it's flexible enough for use on curves.

- CUT STONE set on edge creates an elegant look. The top of the stone should extend 1 or $1^{1}/_{2}$ inches above the gravel or other paving material, and the sides should be butted tightly against the paving material. If you are using mortar between the joints on the path, use it between the edging pieces as well for a uniform appearance.

- BRICK EDGING suits a formal garden as well as a cottage garden. It is easy to install—simply stand bricks on end or place them at a 45-degree angle—but be aware that firm soil is needed to hold the bricks in place. After you've set the edging, pack soil against the outside of the bricks, tamping it firmly in place.

- POURED CONCRETE makes a neat and secure edging. It can be used as a decorative ribbon flush with the path or as an invisible underground edging, as shown at left. However, concrete requires more expertise than other materials and is best installed by a professional.

Installing Lumber Edging

Install your path edgings before laying the setting bed and paving. String mason's line around the path perimeter (see page 115) to mark the exact borders; adjust the line to the height of the edging, 1 inch to $1\frac{1}{2}$ inches above the finished surface of the path.

For straight-edged paths, use 2-by-4 or 2-by-6 lumber set on edge. For curves, use a triple layer of flexible benderboard.

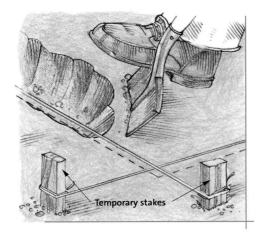

Temporary stakes

1 MAKE A NARROW TRENCH inside the marked perimeter lines to accommodate the edging. It should be deep enough that the top edge of the lumber will just touch the twine.

2 WORKING ON THE OUTSIDE of the perimeter lines, drive in 1-by-3 stakes flush with the lines. Place a stake at each side of a corner, at each joint where two boards meet, and at intervals of 4 feet along the path edge.

3 FASTEN ANY EDGING BOARDS that form a corner. Place all the boards in the trench and attach them to the stakes with nails or screws (see left).

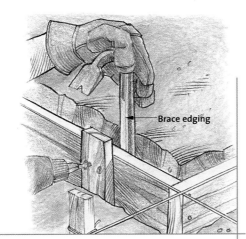

Brace edging

4 SAW OFF THE EXPOSED STAKE SECTIONS at an angle, as shown; then pack the excavated soil to fill in around the outside of the edging.

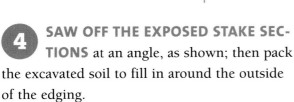

Flagstone Paths

Flagstone occurs naturally in big, flat pieces. Lay it tightly fitted and mortared, and it will look formal enough for an entrance walkway. Or forgo the mortar and allow wide gaps between the stones, and you can tuck plants into the path so that it suits a cottage garden.

OPPOSITE: Flagstone is ideal for level or slightly sloping areas of a hillside garden. For safety reasons, choose a type of stone that isn't likely to become covered with slippery moss.

Shopping for flagstone. When you are shopping for flagstone, choose pieces thick enough for your construction method. For a flagstone path on a bed of gravel and sand, select stone at least $1\frac{1}{2}$ inches thick. For a path to be set in mortar, you can use pieces as thin as 1 inch. As for width, the wider the better—at least a few flagstones 3 feet across or even wider will look wonderful in a path. See pages 132–133 for tips on moving heavy stone pieces.

Flagstone is generally sold by the ton. A ton of stone 2 inches thick generally covers about 70 square feet, or about 20 feet of a $3\frac{1}{2}$-foot-wide path. Bring your path dimensions with you when you go shopping, and ask the stone-yard staff to calculate how much you need. Buy at least 10 percent extra.

Here are some factors to consider:

● IF YOU WANT A NATURAL-LOOKING PATH, choose stone that matches any stone you already have on the site, or stone common to your region. Local stone also may be the least expensive.

● IF YOUR PATH IS SHADED or if you live where it is frequently damp, avoid relatively porous stone, such as some sandstone. It may quickly become covered with slippery moss.

● IF YOU'RE PLANNING OTHER STONE PROJECTS in your garden, see what's available for all your projects before deciding on any one component.

Sand or mortar? A dry-laid flagstone path on a bed of gravel and sand with just sand packed into the joints is the simplest to build; instructions are provided on pages 110–111. Rainwater filters between the stones reasonably well, so usually there's no runoff to cause erosion on a slope. The path surface also remains somewhat flexible; if a tree root or ice pushes up from underneath, you can simply lift a tilted stone and reset it. And with sand joints, you can plant between the stones.

continued ▶▶

That said, there are two good reasons to lay flagstone on mortar with mortar in the joints: no weeds between the stones, and easier maintenance—a mortared flagstone path is simple to sweep or power-spray. But the construction requires more expertise, since the flagstones need to be mortared onto a concrete base. You'll probably want to hire a contractor experienced in building forms and pouring concrete to construct at least the concrete pad.

A third option might seem to offer the best of both methods: build a simple dry-laid path, but instead of packing sand into the joints, spread dry mortar mix into them and then mist with water. However, because this type of path lacks a concrete base, the joints will be weaker. You will most likely need to make annual repairs, especially if you live in an area where the ground freezes. The joints probably won't stand up to pressure-washing, either.

If you decide to mortar the joints of your flagstone path, creating a solid surface, drainage will be affected. Before you start excavating, read about drainage on pages 70–73.

Cut-Stone Paving

Cut stone is stone that has already been sawn into squares and rectangles. It's available in a variety of sizes, thicknesses, and surfaces. Lay it as described on pages 110–111, choosing thick stone for dry-laid paths and thinner stone for use over a mortared bed. Avoid polished stone—it's too slippery to be safely used outdoors. For the most formal look, make the joints small and mortar them. See Chapter 2 for additional paving ideas using cut stone.

Cutting flagstones. It's relatively simple to trim flagstones, either with hand tools or with a power saw or an angle grinder fitted with a diamond blade. Be sure to wear goggles even for small trimming jobs; if you are using power tools, add ear protection and a respirator that blocks fine dust.

The best hand tools for the job are a stone chisel and a stonecutter's hand hammer.

1 **PLACE THE FLAGSTONE** under its neighbor and use a pencil to mark a cutting line for the edge so the two pieces will fit together well.

2 **SCORE A 1/8-INCH-DEEP GROOVE** along the cutting line, using a chisel and hammer.

3 **PLACE A METAL PIPE** under the stone for support, with the waste portion and the scored line overhanging it. Strike the waste portion with the hammer to split the flagstone.

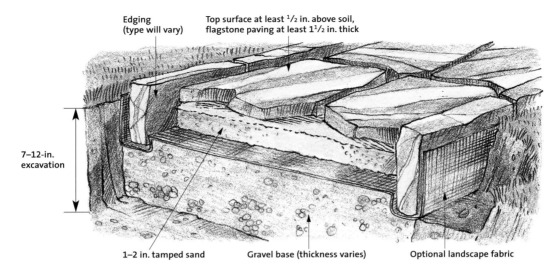

Edging
(type will vary)

Top surface at least $^1/_2$ in. above soil,
flagstone paving at least $1^1/_2$ in. thick

7–12-in.
excavation

1–2 in. tamped sand

Gravel base (thickness varies)

Optional landscape fabric

Laying flagstones in a sand bed. Before you begin excavating for your flagstone path, decide on an edging; some possibilities are shown on pages 104–105. Then follow these steps:

1 MARK THE PATH PERIMETER WITH STAKES and string or washable spray paint. Excavate the entire path area, going down 7 inches where winters are mild, 12 inches where the ground freezes more than a few inches deep. To check the excavation depth, lay a straight piece of lumber across the hole and then measure down from its bottom edge. If you will be installing deep edging, such as stone pavers set vertically, dig straight down along the edges so the pieces will rest against undisturbed soil.

2 ADD 3 INCHES OF GRAVEL. Dampen the gravel, then pack it down with a hand tamper or a motorized plate compactor. Add more gravel in layers of 3 inches or less, leaving room at the top for 1 to 2 inches of sand and the flagstones. Dampen and compact each layer before adding the next.

3 COVER THE GRAVEL WITH LANDSCAPE FABRIC if you decide to use it (see page 102). Install your edging when the gravel base is the appropriate height. Shovel on the sand (use masonry sand or paver base). Rake it into a uniform layer that will compress to the thickness you need.

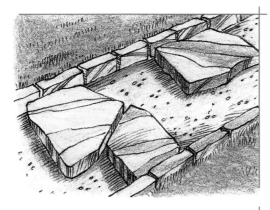

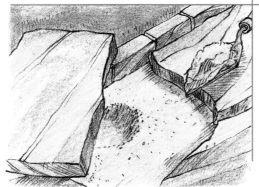

4 **MOVE LARGE STONES INTO THE PATH** and position them where they look good and won't need much trimming. Stones with at least one straight side work well along the path edge. Don't worry about leveling them at this point.

Working on a section perhaps 8 feet long, fill in with smaller flagstones. Make any necessary cuts (see "Cutting Flagstones," page 109). Remove all the flagstones in the section, keeping them in the same arrangement.

5 **REPOSITION THE STONES** one at a time, using a trowel to scrape away or pile up sand until each stone is secure and level with adjacent stones. To avoid having to reposition big stones, smooth the sand slightly higher than you think it needs to be, then remove a handful from the center of the space before you lower the stone; twist the stone until it's firmly set and at the right height. Excess sand will flow into the hole you created under the stone. Check stones frequently with a level.

6 **AS YOU FINISH EACH SECTION,** pack sand into the joints with a short length of ³⁄₈-inch rebar or a scrap of wood.

7 **WHEN ALL THE STONES ARE SET,** sprinkle on more sand or paver base. Sweep or brush it into the crevices and mist the path well. Keep adding, sweeping, and misting until the joints are full. Only at this point is the path firm enough to walk on.

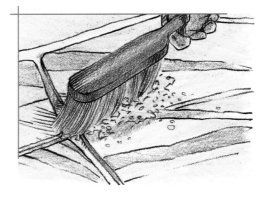

Common brick is well suited to paving because its surface is rough and provides traction. Some bricks withstand cold weather better than others; if you live where it regularly freezes and thaws, be sure to choose an appropriate kind.

Brick and Paver Paths

Like flagstone, bricks and pavers can be laid on a firmly tamped base of gravel and sand with a strong edging. You'll find a dizzying variety of bricks and pavers available. More than anything, though, it's the pattern in which the bricks or pavers are laid that makes the paving interesting; experiment with different arrangements.

Shopping for bricks and pavers. Brick comes in many colors, speckled or multi-hued, used or imitation-used. Concrete pavers are less expensive, but be careful of the faux appearance many of them have; these types do not blend into the landscape very well. Pavers may be round, square, rectangular, or hexagonal; interlocking pavers form a particularly rigid, secure surface.

Thinner pavers are more suitable for mortaring on a concrete pad than for being laid in sand; check with the supplier. If you live where ground regularly freezes and thaws, be sure to buy bricks or pavers that will withstand the climate.

Tightly laid bricks or pavers create a more or less solid surface, so drainage will be affected. Before you start the excavation, read about drainage control on pages 70–73.

Laying brick and pavers. With careful preparation and installation, bricks or pavers that are laid in sand on a level area or slight slope can be as durable as those set in mortar. But be sure to attend to drainage, install firm edgings, and tamp the path base well so that materials stay in position.

The instructions that follow are for a dry-laid brick path; pavers can be laid in exactly the same way.

This brick-in-sand path includes a 3-inch-deep gravel bed, a layer of landscape fabric (optional—see page 102), 1½ to 2 inches of packed masonry sand, and rigid edgings (see pages 104–105). Lay 4 or more inches of gravel if soil drainage is poor, 6 to 8 inches where the ground freezes.

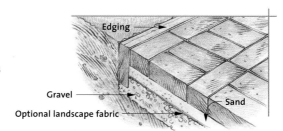

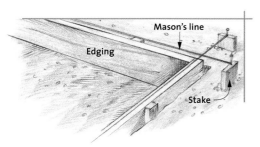

1 **MARK THE PATH PERIMETER** with stakes and mason's line. Excavate the path area (turn to page 117 for guidelines) to make room for the gravel bed, sand, and bricks; install the permanent edging you've chosen. The edgings will serve as good leveling guides for preparing and laying the bricks.

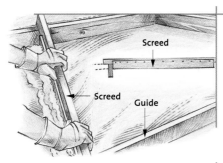

2 **ADD 3 INCHES OF GRAVEL.** Dampen the gravel, then pack it down with a hand tamper or a motorized plate compactor. Add more gravel as needed in layers of 3 inches or less, leaving room at the top for 1½ to 2 inches of sand and the bricks. Dampen and compact each layer before adding the next. Cover the gravel with landscape fabric if you are using it.

Shovel on the sand. Dampen it and level it with a screed, as shown, resting one end of the screed on a temporary guide if necessary.

3 **STRING ANOTHER MASON'S LINE** to help align the courses of bricks. Beginning at one corner, lay bricks tightly against one another, tapping each into place with a hand sledge or mallet. Check frequently that the bricks are level.

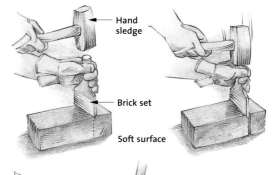

4 **MAKE ANY CUTS** that are necessary for fit. Score a line on all four sides of the brick (near right), then make the cut with one sharp blow (far right). If you need to do a lot of cutting, or shaping of angles, rent a brick saw.

5 **THROW DAMP, FINE SAND** over the finished paving, let it dry for a few hours, and then sweep it into the joints. Spray the path lightly with water so that the sand settles completely.

PATIOS

FROM A CONSTRUCTION STANDPOINT, A PATIO IS ESSENTIALLY THE SAME AS A PATH—AND IN FACT, some patios aren't much larger than a generous path. As with a path, consider drainage as you plan your patio. If you want an outdoor kitchen, be sure to lay whatever pipes you need for gas, electricity, or plumbing before you install the patio's gravel base.

ABOVE: Finding just the right flat space for a patio can be difficult on some hillside lots. You can cut into the hillside to expand your patio area, but don't build on top of fill unless you work with a professional to secure the filled area.

Patio Paving Materials

Any paving you use for a path can be used for a patio. A poured-concrete patio is usually a job for a professional, but concrete pavers, bricks, and stones are easy to work with. Before you make your decision, check pages 12–65 for ideas. Also consider these practical points:

● PAVING OVER TREE ROOTS may irreparably damage some trees. If you can't avoid placing the patio over a tree's root zone, choose a permeable paving such as gravel, bricks, or flagstone on sand so that air and water can get to the roots.

● IF YOU PLAN TO HAVE PATIO FURNITURE, consider how smooth the surface needs to be. Delicate metal chairs with tiny feet may necessitate the use of large cut-stone pieces with joints that are either very narrow or filled with mortar. But if you have wooden furniture with thick legs, other paving choices may be fine.

Excavating for a Patio

Once you decide on a paving material, you can build a patio using the same basic steps as for a path (see pages 98–113). The excavation process is a little different, however, because provisions for grading to facilitate drainage are more critical.

The following directions are for a patio off a house. In this situation, it's vital that water is carefully drained away from the house. For more information about drainage, see pages 70–73.

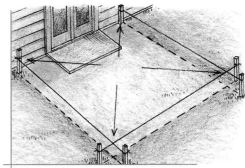

1 **DRIVE STAKES INTO THE GROUND** and tie on string to mark the area you want to excavate. Keep the stakes back a bit, as shown, so they aren't in your way as you dig and build the patio. If you are using edging that will be held in place with stakes, give yourself room to install them by placing the string at least 8 inches beyond the eventual patio edges. Otherwise, adjust the placement for the type of edging you are using (see pages 104–105).

To be sure the corners are at right angles, measure from each stake next to the house to the corner diagonally across from it. The two distances should be equal.

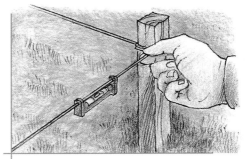

2 **MARK THE EVENTUAL PATIO HEIGHT** on a stake close to the house. Adjust the string to that mark. Slip a line level over the string; at the stake away from the house, raise or lower the string until it is level. Mark that height on the second stake. Repeat the process to mark all the stakes.

3 **DIVIDE THE DISTANCE** the patio extends out from the house, measured in feet, by 8. The result is the number of inches the patio must slope to ensure good drainage. On the outer stakes, measure down by this amount from your first marks. This is the finished elevation.

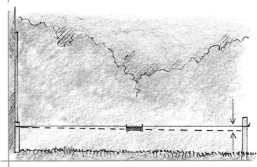

4 **USING THESE REFERENCE POINTS,** you can excavate soil to the correct depth, add a precise thickness of base materials, and install edging to align correctly with the finished patio surface. If the patio is large, you might need additional reference lines: just add more stakes and string every 5 feet or so.

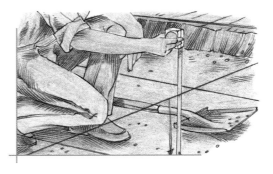

water
features and
boulders

WATER ANIMATES A HILLSIDE BY ITS SOUND
AND BY ITS MOVEMENT OVER THE LAND. IT
ALSO DRAWS THE EYE TO THE BANK OR HILLTOP
FROM WHICH IT SPRINGS, THE LITTLE CANYON
THROUGH WHICH IT FLOWS. BOULDERS, TOO,
CALL ATTENTION TO PLACE, SHOWING WHAT
THE HILLSIDE IS MADE OF THROUGH THEIR
PARTICULAR COLORS AND STRIATIONS.

PONDS

A SIMPLE POND IS SIMPLE TO BUILD. Place it downslope, where water would naturally pool, and edge it with a beach or boulders, or both; or have a flagstone patio extend right to the water's edge. To learn how to prevent water from running off the slope into the pond or pooling under it, see page 73.

Choose low (almost flat) or dome-shaped boulders to place around your pond. These shapes are naturally widest at the base, so they will look stable and solid when settled only an inch or two into the soil.

Flexible Liner or Shell?

The most common basic options for do-it-yourself pond builders are flexible liners and rigid preformed shells made of fiberglass or polyethylene. (Concrete is an alternative, but it is both complicated and expensive.) Shells are really no easier to install than flexible liners—large shells are, in fact, more difficult— and they offer limited shapes and may look artificial. The directions provided in this book are for flexible-liner ponds.

Made of a rubberlike material, flexible liners can fit just about any size and shape of pond you desire. The drawback with a flexible liner is that you must be careful not to puncture it. Purchase a thick, durable liner, such as one made of 45-mil EPDM (ethylene propylene diene monomer), and protect it with carpet scraps or liner protection fabric specially designed for garden ponds.

Installing a Flexible-Liner Pond

Decide how deep you are going to make your pond. A pond with plants or fish needs to be at least 18 inches deep, or 24 inches if you live in a cold-winter climate and want to overwinter plants in the pond. Plan your pond's shape and dimensions as well.

Liner and liner protection fabric should be large enough to extend 1 foot beyond the pond edges, where they can be covered with pebbles, boulders, or flagstone. To both the width and length of the pond, add these minimum amounts for overlap and a reasonable margin of error: if your pond is 18 inches at its deepest point, add 4 feet to width and length; if your pond is 24 inches deep, add 5 feet; if it's 30 inches deep, add 6 feet. Allow for any shelves you plan for the pond edge.

1 **MARK THE POND OUTLINE** with flour, sand, or spray paint. Excavate to the desired depth, setting aside the topsoil. For a marginal shelf on which to place pebbles, boulders, or potted plants, excavate 6 to 12 inches below grade, outline the shelf (make it at least 10 inches wide, up to 24 inches for large pots), and then finish the pond excavation to the desired depth. Slope the sides of the shelf if you think it might crumble.

To check the depth of the excavation, lay a 2 by 4 across the hole and measure from the bottom of the hole to the bottom of the 2 by 4. Make sure the pond edges are level by setting a carpenter's level on the 2 by 4. If necessary, fill any dips in the edges with some of the excavated soil, tamping it down well.

2 **LINE THE HOLE** with liner protection fabric. If the bottom surface is full of sharp rocks, you may want to dig 2 inches deeper and add sand before installing the liner protection fabric. With the aid of a helper if the pond is large, spread the liner across the hole (warming the liner in the sun first makes it more flexible). Adjust the liner to follow the contours of the hole as closely as possible. Carefully pull and smooth the liner to reduce the size and number of creases.

continued ▶▶

3 **ANCHOR THE EDGES TEMPORARILY** with heavy stones and slowly fill the pond with water from a garden hose. As it fills, wade in and work on smoothing out the creases; lift the stones to relieve any tension on the liner and allow it to settle. Some creases are inevitable, but try to minimize them.

For a natural look, place a few rocks and pebbles in the pond or on the pond shelf, rinsing any dirt off them first. Allow the filled pond to settle for a week before you trim the liner and install the edging stone.

Boulder Edging

The edge of a steep-sided pond made with a liner may not be sufficiently sturdy to take the weight of a boulder without caving in and letting soil slide under the liner. Supporting the edge with concrete block or a concrete collar is one solution, but a simpler option is to place the boulder outside the pond edging or inside the pond itself rather than on the rim.

Boulders can sit on the pond bottom or on a marginal shelf if it's sufficiently stable. Place liner protection fabric on the pond liner beneath each boulder. Be extremely careful not to rip the liner on the side of the pond while installing the boulders; settle them into a bed of rounded gravel if they have sharp edges or need stabilizing.

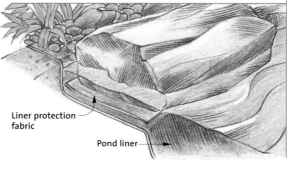

Liner protection fabric

Pond liner

Boulders are best positioned in the pond or outside it, not on the pond edge.

Paving the Pond Edge

If you're thinking of edging your pond with paving stone, such as flagstone or cut stone, consider whether people will be walking to the water's edge. If the answer is yes, for safety's sake choose extra-large stone (say, 3 feet by 3 feet) so weight is distributed away from the pond edge. If your soil is unstable, consider having a 4-inch-thick reinforced concrete footing poured around the pond, or at least the section where there will be access, to support the paving stones.

The method described here for paving stone can also be used to set fieldstones and pebbles. But be careful not to ring the pond with an unnatural-looking "necklace" of small stones.

Let the water-filled pond settle for a week before laying the stone edge.

Japanese iris plants love water. For information about water-garden plants and water gardening, see pages 158–159.

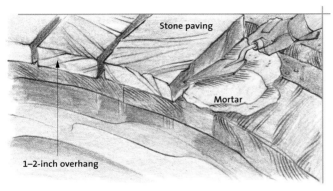

Stone paving

Mortar

1–2-inch overhang

① WITH THE POOL FILLED, trim the liner to 4 or 5 inches past the pond edge. Lay a dry run of stones, each one overhanging the pond rim by 1 to 2 inches. Do any necessary cutting of the stone (see page 109) so the edging fits perfectly. Mix mortar, spread a 1-inch-thick layer on the pond edge, and set the stones in place. (If you buy a premixed mortar that contains lime, be careful not to spill any in the water, because lime fouls pond water.)

② BED EACH STONE FIRMLY in position by tapping it with a rubber mallet. Use a straightedge (a long piece of straight 2 by 4) and a carpenter's level to check that the edging is even from one side of the pond to the other. Clean any mortar splashes from the stones with a sponge and water as you work.

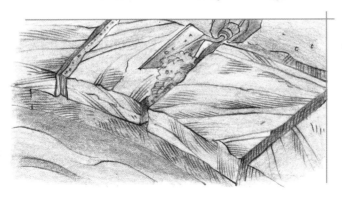

③ LET THE SPREAD MORTAR SET for 24 hours. Then make a fresh mortar mix and pack mortar between the stones. Smooth the joints with a pointed trowel. Keep off the edging for three days to let the mortar harden.

FOUNTAINS AND SPRINGS

INSTALL A SPRING TOWARD THE BASE OF A BANK OR BUBBLING UP OVER ROCK ANYWHERE ON THE HILLSIDE—someplace a spring might emerge in nature. If a tall jet fountain is what you have in mind, its logical location is downhill, where the force of gravity on water draining down the slope might have caused it naturally. In a windy location, choose a fountain nozzle with a low spray pattern rather than a tall jet so that the water won't fly away.

In this spill fountain, water drops from one barrel into another. The pump is in the bottom barrel; the tubing to the top barrel is hidden behind luxuriant foliage.

The Mechanics of Moving Water

A fountain or spring is composed of a reservoir of water (either a pond or a container hidden beneath rocks) and a pump that sits in the water. A cable goes from the pump out over the side of the water reservoir to a waterproof outdoor electrical outlet.

There are two main types of fountains: jets of water that spray or bubble up from the reservoir, and sheets of water that typically splash from the top of a statue or out of a chute. For a jet, a fountainhead nozzle is screwed onto the pump itself. For the sheet effect, water is carried from the reservoir to the top of the statue or chute by plastic tubing attached to the flow outlet on the pump.

Consult a pump supplier about a suitable pump for the fountain or spring you have in mind. The larger the water flow and the greater the head (the vertical distance from the surface of the water reservoir to the top of the jet or chute), the bigger the pump you will need. Be sure the pump's electrical cable is long enough to reach from the bottom of the water reservoir to the electrical outlet.

If there's not a nearby GFCI electrical outlet (ground fault circuit interrupter—it will interrupt the flow of electricity if there is a fault, or break, in the circuit), have an electrician install one. Where the cable crosses the garden, run it through 1-inch PVC pipe and bury it in the ground to keep it safe from the blade of a spade or a child's toy.

Making a Pebble Fountain

Putting together a fountain out of pebbles or small stones is relatively easy. Make the water reservoir using a black liner, a preformed pond shell, or any kind of large, watertight container at least 15 inches deep. The reservoir can be anywhere from 18 to 36 inches wide— or even wider. The larger the reservoir, the less frequently you will have to refill it.

Mesh square

Pebbles

To GFCI outlet

Wire mesh

Flexible liner

Pump

Reservoir

Brick

1 PLACE THE PUMP IN THE RESERVOIR on top of a clean brick so the silt that collects on the reservoir bottom can't enter the pump. Fit a rigid extension pipe to the pump outlet and screw the fountain nozzle onto the top of the pipe. The nozzle should sit above the top of the reservoir so the spray will fan over the stones, as shown. Trim the extension pipe or raise the pump as needed to achieve the correct height. Take the electrical cable out over the edge of the reservoir in the direction of the GFCI outlet, burying it in PVC pipe.

2 PLACE A PIECE OF STRONG, rustproof wire mesh over the reservoir, making sure it overlaps the edges by at least 6 inches on all sides. Cut out an access hole large enough to put your hand through comfortably, so that you can reach the pump to adjust the water flow or clear the filter screen. Place a square of mesh over the cutout, large enough not to sag through the hole once it's covered with pebbles.

3 FILL THE RESERVOIR with water. Place a few larger stones on the edges of the wire mesh to secure it, then cover the rest of the mesh with pebbles. Mark the access hole with a few highly colored or glass pebbles. Plug in the pump to check the jet spray. Adjust the water flow if necessary to ensure that the spray stays within the stone-covered area and drips back into the reservoir. During hot or windy weather, check that the water level has not dropped below the pump; refill the reservoir if necessary.

Stones are sometimes available predrilled for a fountain pipe. You can do the job yourself if you have the patience: rent a hammer drill and use a masonry bit. Wear ear protectors and goggles.

A Natural Spring

This attractive combination of pipes seems entirely natural because of its assumed practical purpose, to drain rainwater off the steep bank. However, all the water is recycled from a pond below. There's a pump there, with an electrical cable that plugs into a GFCI outlet nearby; plastic tubing runs from the pump up the hillside, through plantings, into the metal pipe.

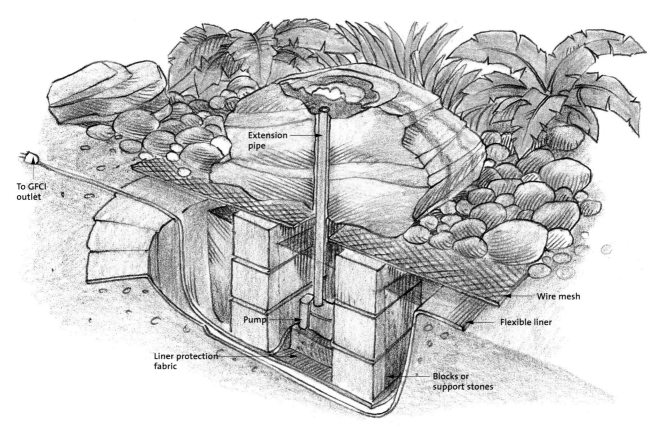

Extension pipe

To GFCI outlet

Pump

Liner protection fabric

Wire mesh

Flexible liner

Blocks or support stones

Installing a Boulder Spring

Installing a boulder spring is similar to making a pebble fountain, as outlined on page 123. Some suppliers of stone boulders sell stones already drilled for a fountain pipe, or they will drill the boulder of your choice.

1 **MAKE A WATER RESERVOIR** as described for a pebble fountain. Then install liner protection fabric on the reservoir bottom and stack up two columns of concrete blocks or flat stones on the fabric to support the boulder.

2 **PLACE THE PUMP ON A BRICK** between the columns, screw an extension pipe onto the pump outlet, and install wire mesh over the reservoir. If you want the fountain to gurgle and bubble out of the top of the pipe (as shown) rather than form a spray pattern, you don't need a fountain nozzle.

3 **LOWER THE BOULDER INTO POSITION,** making sure it is well supported by the two columns. Complete as for a pebble fountain, arranging pebbles around the boulder.

STREAMS AND DRY CREEKBEDS

BUILDING A NATURAL-LOOKING STREAM IS A TWO-PART UNDERTAKING: mimicking how water flows in nature, and making a waterproof channel to keep the water from escaping. The work is reduced by half if you build a dry creekbed; and if you choose and place stones well, you'll almost be able to hear water chuckle and splash in it.

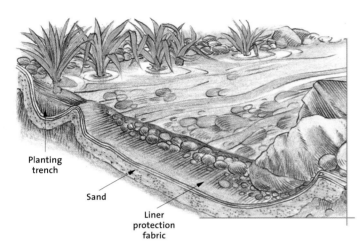

Planting trench

Sand

Liner protection fabric

Shaping a Watercourse

In nature, water either flows downhill through gently sloping valleys or spills off a rock ledge, collects in a pool, and then overflows into a stream. The stream widens at bends, turning around a rock promontory and leaving a shallow beach downstream on the outside curve. Boulders too big to roll with the current stay in the middle of the stream, while smaller ones wash to the sides to lie half-buried in silt. In most streams, there are places where water slows and collects in deep pools and other places where it ripples over rocky shallow stretches or rushes through a gorge.

Try to make the line of your stream convey this sense of natural water movement. For more guidelines, see pages 58–59.

Building a Stream

To build a stream, you'll need a waterproof channel, an uphill water source, and a downhill pond or collection tank in which a pump is positioned. The pump connects to two things: a plastic pipe that delivers water back up to the top of the stream, and a GFCI electrical outlet (see "The Mechanics of Moving Water," page 122). The pond or tank needs to be large enough to hold all the water that drains from the stream when the pump is turned off.

For the water source at the top of the stream, you can create a spring or have water spill from a pond, perhaps over a waterfall. Downhill, a stream typically slips into a pool or disappears into a pipe to an underground reservoir. Install both the downhill pond and the uphill water source before you build the stream.

Select or build a mild slope so water won't rush down too fast; a 1 or 2 percent grade is about right. You can make a concrete channel or use a flexible liner, as described here, but a flexible liner will take a lot less work.

1 **EXCAVATE THE STREAMBED** to a depth of 6 inches for the shallow stretches, 10 inches for the occasional deep pools (water will collect here when the pump is turned off). To allow for plants, dig shallow trenches on the side of the streambed, as shown above. Make the streambed wide enough to accommodate rocks and pebbles, which will help hide the liner. To add a small waterfall, see pages 128–131.

2 LINE THE STREAMBED EXCAVATION with 3 inches of damp sand and a layer of liner protection fabric; then install the liner itself and another layer of liner protection fabric. Place stones, gravel, and sand in a natural-looking arrangement in and along the watercourse. Plant marginal or bog plants (see pages 156–159) in soil in the trenches.

3 PLACE A PUMP in the bottom of your downhill pond or tank. Run the electrical cable to a nearby GFCI outlet, burying it in PVC pipe. Run flexible vinyl tubing (sold at pond supply stores) from the pump uphill to the source of the stream, burying it in PVC pipe or taking it on the ground among plants. Turn on the pump and experiment with rock placement until you are pleased with the look and sound of the stream.

Check for leaks by looking for moist areas on the stream bank or a lower water level in the downhill pond when the pump is off. Then finish the edging, disguising the liner with overhanging rocks or a layer of sand or gravel.

Making a Dry Creekbed

The most natural-looking location for a dry creekbed is along a depression or trough already formed by runoff. Or start your creekbed at the "outfall," or open end, of the pipe in a French drain (see page 72) so water will funnel into the creekbed during rainstorms.

Plan the course of a dry creekbed to look realistic (see "Shaping a Watercourse," opposite). Then excavate the creekbed to the desired depth and width. To use it as a drainage channel, bury 4-inch perforated drainpipe—holes facing downward—in the center of the creekbed with the outflow directed to a storm drain. Edge and fill the creekbed with smooth-edged river rock, water-tumbled boulders, and polished gravel. Settle the larger rocks into the banks.

Unlike a stream intended to hold water, a dry creekbed doesn't need a waterproof lining. In fact, during wet weather it's usually desirable to let the water soak into the ground.

Partially buried border stones

Loose rocks and gravel

4-inch perforated drainpipe (optional)

To storm drain or other disposal area

WATERFALLS

A HILLSIDE GARDEN OFFERS EXCELLENT OPPORTUNITIES TO SHOWCASE FALLING WATER. Break the fall into stages, or stair steps, or have the water drop all at once in a dramatic plunge. Start by surveying the inclines and outcroppings in your garden, imagining what they would look like with water coursing down them.

OPPOSITE: Increasing the height of a waterfall increases the sound of the splash. To make an even bigger splash, position a rock at the base of the falls to break up the water. A series of falls makes for a pleasing variety of sounds.

Components of a Waterfall

A waterfall consists of a water source such as a small pond at the top of the fall, a series of rocks or a single large rock over which the water tumbles, and a pond or collection tank below the fall. In the lower pond or tank is a pump that connects to two things: a plastic pipe that delivers water back up to the source, and a GFCI outlet nearby in the garden (see "The Mechanics of Moving Water," page 122). For options in materials, see "Leakproofing a Waterfall" on page 131. For help in creating natural stone arrangements, consult pages 56–57 and look through nature books.

SPILL STONE

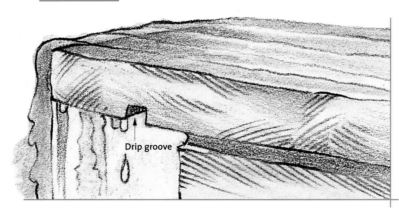

Drip groove

WEIR

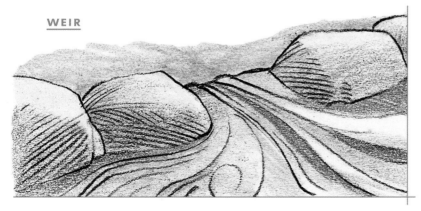

Spill Stone or Weir?

At the top of a waterfall, the water either slips over a spill stone or is channeled through a weir.

With a spill stone, its shape and lip configuration determine the fall pattern. A wide, rectangular stone with a smooth lip produces a neat curtain of water, while a stone with a jagged lip creates multiple streams. The spill stone may be cantilevered over a backing stone; a small groove cut on the underside of the spill stone, parallel to its lip, will prevent water from dripping backward and spoiling the effect.

Instead of having a spill stone, you can position a stone on each side of the channel at the edge of the falls, leaving a gap—a weir—through which the water flows to drop to the level below.

Building a Simple Waterfall

The simplest waterfall is a single-step fall, with water flowing from an upper pond or stream over a spill stone into a lower pond. In a modest-size garden, such an arrangement is far more credible, visually, than a towering cascade. And the sound is more soothing.

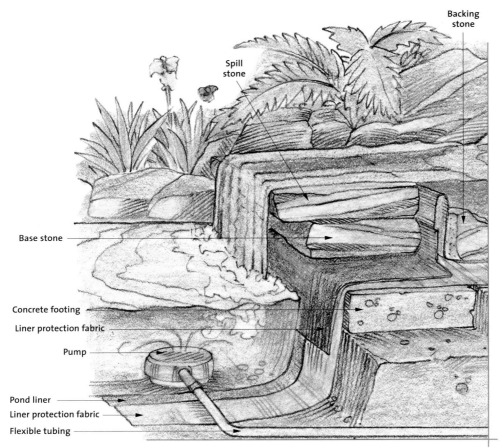

Backing stone

Spill stone

Base stone

Concrete footing

Liner protection fabric

Pump

Pond liner

Liner protection fabric

Flexible tubing

1 **EXCAVATE THE LOWER POND,** making it significantly larger than the upper one will be. (For information on building a pond, see pages 118–121.) As you lay the liner protection fabric and the pond liner, leave plenty of both in the waterfall area so you can bring them up behind the spill stone and other rocks, as shown at left.

2 **MAKE A FIRM SHELF** above the lower pond for the spill stone and its base stone. The stones must be secure: if the soil is soft, reinforce the shelf with small stones set in the soil or, if the waterfall stones are very heavy, with concrete block or a 4-inch concrete footing, as shown.

3 **PLACE A PIECE OF LINER PROTECTION FABRIC** on the shelf, over the liner. Then position the waterfall base stone and spill stone on the shelf, settling the base stone into a bed of gravel if it has sharp edges.

4 **STACK TALLER ROCKS** on each side of the waterfall stones to channel the water and give a sense that water scoured a gorge through bedrock. Place liner protection fabric beneath the rocks and ensure that each rock is stable before placing the next one.

5 CREASE THE LINER behind the waterfall so that the waterproofing extends almost to the top of the spill stone, as shown. Use a backing stone to anchor the liner so that the crease stays in place.

6 EXCAVATE AND LINE the upper pond. Place a pump in the lower pond and run the electrical cable to a nearby GFCI outlet (see page 122). Run flexible vinyl tubing from the pump up to the upper pond (or stream source), burying it in PVC pipe or laying it on the ground among plants. Fill the ponds with water.

7 TURN ON THE PUMP and run the waterfall to check rock placement and water flow. The spill stone may need adjusting so that the water spills off its edge in a sheet. Tilting it forward or making a groove on the underside will help create a proper spill. While you have the water running, check for leaks, especially where liner pieces overlap; look for moist areas on the stream bank or a lower water level in the downhill pond when the pump is off. If necessary, seal pieces with seam tape recommended for flexible liners.

8 ONCE THE ROCKS SEEM WELL PLACED and the sound of the water is pleasant, shut off the pump and mortar the gaps between the rocks by the falls so water cannot flow beneath them. Apply a waterproof sealer to the mortar and finish the pond edgings (see pages 120–121).

Leakproofing a Waterfall

It's crucial that the entire waterfall structure—upper and lower reservoirs, falls, and splash zone—be waterproof. You can choose a flexible liner, free-form concrete, fiberglass shells, a series of spill pans, or a combination of these materials.

Concrete allows you to sculpt the water channel most freely, but it requires steel reinforcement—either reinforcing bar or wire mesh—and tends to develop cracks eventually; professionals often place liner beneath the concrete.

Great care must be taken not to pierce a liner while positioning rocks. Between rocks or between rocks and the liner, you can use mortar; color it black or gray to make it nearly invisible.

BOULDERS

INSTALLING BOULDERS ON A HILLSIDE
IS VIGOROUS, HEAVY, AND TRICKY WORK.
Chances are the job is bigger than you think;
you'll need fair-sized rock even for a small project, and moving rock up or
down a hill requires great attention to safety. You may want to plan on getting help from a contractor recommended by your rock yard.

Working with Professionals

If you plan to install boulders on a slope, consult a geotechnical engineer
or landscape architect to ascertain whether the slope can hold the rocks
securely. You might also show a landscape architect or garden designer your
plans, to avoid installing a 2-ton rock in the wrong place. Find someone
who has a record of doing excellent rock installations.

Most yards will deliver rock in a dump truck, leaving it for you to put
in place. If you are installing rock in a flat area, you might consider renting
a skid-steer loader with a backhoe and a bucket attachment (look in the
Yellow Pages under "Contractors' Equipment and Supplies"). If the terrain
is even gently sloping, however, have the rock delivered to the site and leave
it to professionals to operate the equipment. For big rocks, find a yard that

ABOVE: Once they are in
place, large rocks look
better than small ones.
To naturalize a new
installation, let creeping
plants sprawl over the
rock edges; many plants
of the same type will
form what looks like a
natural community. For
more information on
placing boulders, see
pages 46–49.

has a boom-equipped truck; you'll want the delivery people to dig holes and set each rock in place.

When you arrange for delivery, be prepared to discuss the location of power lines, overhanging trees, and buried pipes or septic tank as well as the degree of slope and access to the boulder sites. Consider asking for a rock-yard employee to visit your site before delivery to verify that their equipment will work on your hillside.

Take snapshots of the rocks you pick out at the yard, and then decide exactly where and how you want each one placed before the delivery truck arrives. Make dummy rocks—garbage bags filled with newspaper—to help you decide on the final placement. If you start to excavate before the boulders arrive, don't dig too deep; you don't want uncompacted fill beneath a boulder.

Safety First

Transport rock in a cart rather than a single-wheel wheelbarrow, because the weight could easily shift and tip over a barrow. Be careful: it's easy to lose control of a cartful of rock on even a slight slope. If you are installing several boulders on a hillside, start at the foot of the slope. Embed each rock securely, back and down into the slope, before moving uphill.

Wear leather gloves and sturdy boots, and stand to the side of a rock as you're moving it so that if it rolls, it won't roll into you. To lift a small rock without injuring yourself, bend your knees, keeping your back straight, hold the load firmly, and then straighten your knees, keeping your elbows close to your sides. Never try to lift a rock that's too heavy for you; instead, roll it up a plank set on an incline and lever it into a cart.

Moving Boulders by Hand

Carrying rock up or down a hillside is a strenuous task. Most people can't shift rocks that weigh more than 50 to 100 pounds, even on flat ground. For a hillside, because of the risk that a boulder might roll, you'll want to have large rock delivered right to the spot where you are installing it.

If you are moving rocks by yourself, push or drag them with poles and ropes or with boards as shown at right. Use a piece of carpet instead of a board if the rocks have moss or lichen that might get scratched, and place carpet pads beneath ropes to avoid scuffs. Once a boulder is in the hole you've prepared, a rock bar—a thick iron bar with a handle at least 4 feet long—is useful if you need to turn it a few degrees. Have a supply of small rocks on hand to wedge the boulder into position once you're satisfied with its placement.

Artificial Rock

If site conditions make it impossible to install natural rock, consider a concrete product shaped, textured, and colored to resemble natural stone. Artificial rock can be used for individual boulders, steps, waterfalls, and ponds, and also to mask retaining walls. It may cost slightly more than real stone.

Making a Rocky Outcropping

A natural gentle slope is an ideal spot for an outcropping of boulders. As you design the grouping and shop for the rock, bear in mind that a range of rock sizes, including one or two large boulders, makes for a more effective composition than all small stones; and native stone will always look more harmonious than stone from another region.

To mimic a natural outcropping, lay stones in one or more bands, like strata, with the longest side of each stone parallel to the direction of the band. Group stones to avoid a "raisin-cookie" effect—small rocks dotted about the slope. Place large boulders first, and then scatter the smallest rocks at their feet as if they had chipped and fallen off the big rocks.

Some fieldstones, especially those of volcanic origin, can be difficult to compose into a very natural-looking group. Start by finding a rock's flattest side and placing that upward. Position stones so the grain, if they have one, runs the same way in all of them. Settle the stones into the earth; the general rule is to sink a stone into the ground just beyond its widest point. Keep the tops of the stones on the same plane, either horizontal or tilted slightly upward, all at the same angle.

LEFT: Lay boulders in parallel bands, tilting all their tops at the same angle.

Creating a Rock Garden

Natural rock gardens are found on deep piles of fragmented stone at the bases of cliffs or on mountain ridges where alpine plants enjoy the fast-draining soil. You can create your own version of a rock garden as part of your hillside landscaping.

Site your rock garden on a gentle slope, if you can. If your soil is already fast-draining at all times, you don't need the 18-inch excavation described below. Install your boulders and then excavate to a depth of 1 inch before planting and laying the gravel surface.

1 **MARK OUT YOUR GARDEN AREA.** Place a group of boulders at the top edge, arranging them like a natural outcropping (see facing page), with their steepest, most clifflike sides toward the planting site. Be sure the tops all tilt at the same angle. Excavate the remaining planting area to a depth of 18 inches.

2 **SPREAD A 6-INCH LAYER OF DRAINAGE MATERIAL—** rocks, broken bricks, chunks of old concrete, or equal parts gravel and sand—in the excavation. Then fill to within 1 inch of the surface level with a fast-draining soil mix of 1 part crushed rock ($^1/_2$- or $^3/_4$-inch size with smaller particles included) or pea gravel, 1 part coarse sand, and 2 parts good garden soil. Some rock gardeners prefer far more crushed rock, but that means the mix will dry out more quickly and you will need to water more often.

Plant the garden using rock-garden plants; see pages 152–155. Finish your rock garden by spreading 1 inch of gravel on the surface. For a natural look, choose gravel that matches the color of the boulders.

Found Boulders

This hillside patio was brought to the boulders, not the boulders to the patio. Seize the opportunity offered by any boulder that already exists in your garden. Excavate around it to show it to its best advantage, prune a tree to frame it, and make a path to its base. Be sure there's access to its face, because visitors will want to lean against it or touch the warm, rough sides. And a place to sit—that's necessary too.

growing
hillside
plants

ROLLING LAND HAS CHARACTER. AS YOU WORK IT, YOU'LL GET
TO KNOW THE SOIL'S "ANGLE OF REPOSE" (HOW STEEP IT CAN
BE BEFORE IT STARTS TO SLIP) AND FEEL GRAVITY TUGGING AT
YOUR PLANTS AND YOUR WHEELBARROW. GARDENING
ON A SLOPE IS A PRACTICE IN BUILDING STABILITY
AND AVOIDING EROSION.

HILLSIDE MICROCLIMATES

HILLSIDE GARDENS HAVE DISTINCT MICROCLIMATES—AREAS THAT ARE MORE OR LESS WINDY, SUNNY AND warm, or shady and cool. A combination of factors, including garden topography and the location of the house and other structures, creates these variations. Being aware of your site's climatic differences will help you in your planning, from deciding on the most comfortable spot for a sitting area to ensuring that vegetables and roses get enough sunlight.

Shelter from Wind

Hilltops and exposed areas on a hillside tend to be buffeted by winds. Gentle breezes are refreshing during hot weather, but strong winds or even gusts make a patio unappealing. Wind also dries out plants, blows fountain and irrigation water off course, and can snap tree branches.

To deal with wind, you might want to follow the lead of this rooftop garden. Its clear glass barriers block wind without obscuring the view.

If your patio cannot be sited in a sheltered area, grow a windbreak. Planted perpendicular to the prevailing winds, a line of trees or shrubs can reduce wind by as much as 50 percent. The ideal plant windbreak consists of fairly fast-growing, upright trees or shrubs that can be planted close together. Suitable species include some eucalyptus, junipers, pines, pittosporums, privets, and poplars. They don't need to be planted right at the patio edge, where they might cast too much shade. Studies show that in a residential area, maximum wind reduction extends for a distance four times the height of the tallest tree.

To protect a view or to conserve space, you might consider clear glass panels—but be aware that plants are actually better at diffusing wind. Wind tends to drop back down close behind a solid barrier.

In windy parts of the garden, be sure to properly stake and tie newly planted trees. To prevent winds from drying out the soil, mulch around plants with bark chips. Use landscape fabric or chicken wire, pegged at the corners, to hold down the mulch. Install drip irrigation or use low sprinklers to water plants in windy areas; see pages 140–143.

Cold Air and Sunlight

Cold air flows downhill like water, making the lowest parts of a sloping garden the coolest. If a fence or house wall runs at right angles to the slope, air flowing down will collect in a cold pocket against the wall. Be careful not to place garden seating there, or plants that are frost-tender or need warmth.

Another unfavorable spot for marginally hardy plants or seating areas is any stretch of ground exposed to air on all sides (especially the north) and to open sky. In the evening, warmth stored in the ground during the day rises and is quickly replaced by cold air. You can slow the cooling with large-canopied trees or overhead structures that will trap the rising air.

How much sun a site receives depends on its orientation. A north-facing garden area gets the least, a south-facing one the most. An east-facing site receives only morning sun, while a west-facing garden gets the full force of the afternoon sun. A slope intensifies these differences. Tilted toward the sun, a south-facing slope warms up rapidly in spring, giving vegetables or flowers a jump on the season. A north-facing slope is angled away from the sun, so it's a poor place for heat-loving plants and also for seating, except in very warm weather.

An overhead canopy creates a microclimate, intercepting the heat rising from the ground at day's end and thus delaying evening chill.

Cold air flows downhill

Cold air pools here

Cold air pools here

Cold air pools here

LEFT: In a windswept site, a young tree's roots may need anchoring. Sink stakes in a line at right angles to the prevailing wind so they extend only a foot above the ground, as shown. Use ties that won't bind or cut into the bark, such as wide strips of canvas or rubber; fasten each tie around the tree and stake in a figure-8 pattern. The tree should be able to move about an inch in either direction. Remove the ties as soon as the tree appears to be self-supporting, after a year or so.

IRRIGATING A SLOPE

APPLIED TOO HEAVILY OR TOO QUICKLY, IRRIGATION WATER WILL RUN OFF A SLOPE—NOT JUST WASTING the water (often before it gets to plant roots) but also eroding the soil. As you plan your irrigation, try to ensure that no more water will be applied than the soil can absorb.

A SIMPLE SOIL TEST

If you're uncertain what type of soil you have, do a simple test by wetting some soil and squeezing it into a ball. If it crumbles, your soil is sandy. If it sticks firmly together, it's clay. If the ball holds its shape but breaks apart easily, you have loam.

This underground lawn sprinkler system consists of rotary heads (rotors) that spray in an overlapping pattern.

Assessing Your Soil

Soils don't all absorb water the same way. While all soil contains the same ingredients—mineral particles, living and dead organic matter, and pore spaces for water and air—the proportions differ. Knowing your soil type will help you manage your irrigation efficiently.

"Light" soil is sandy, with large pore spaces that let water enter easily and move through quickly. Runoff is unlikely, but you must water frequently to keep the soil from drying out. But be careful not to over-water; the excess will wash down beneath plant roots and be wasted.

Clay soil, often referred to as "heavy" soil, has little pore space. It absorbs moisture slowly, so irrigation water may puddle and run off unless it's applied slowly. However, plants growing in clay can go longer between watering—keep that in mind lest you overwater.

Loam is the ideal soil; it is easy to wet and dries out at a moderate rate. Water spreads slowly and evenly through loam.

On a hillside, soil may be shallow and lie over impermeable rock. In that situation, apply water gently and slowly, because the soil (regardless of type) will become saturated quickly. Then water will run off—taking soil with it.

Averting Runoff

Plants on slopes can be challenging to irrigate because gravity may tug water downhill faster than it can seep into the root zone. To minimize runoff, try these strategies (also see page 69):

• RUN WATER TO TEST how long it takes
for runoff to occur. Always irrigate just short of that time. If your plants require more water, pulse-irrigate: water in short cycles, leaving time in between for the moisture to soak in.

- SLOW DOWN THE DELIVERY RATE. Drip irrigation, with its individual emitters and microsprays, has an output rate as low as half a gallon per hour, compared to the gallons per minute of traditional sprinklers. If you opt for a sprinkler system, consider rotary heads, which dispense water more slowly than spray heads. When hand watering, keep the faucet on low.
- BUILD BASINS AND TERRACES TO CHANNEL WATER to plant roots. These are useful even with a drip or sprinkler system, but to avoid disfiguring the hillside you may want to limit basins to large plants with big root systems. To hand-water large shrubs or trees, attach a deep-root irrigator to the hose.

INDIVIDUAL BASIN	TERRACES

Build up the soil on the downhill side of the plant so that any water running down the slope will pool inside the basin and soak into the plant's root zone.

Install a low retaining wall of boards (see page 85) across the slope near the edge of the root zone and add soil to within a couple of inches of the board top. Be careful not to change the soil level substantially over the roots of an existing plant or to pile soil against the stem.

Watering Options

The three basic options for keeping plants irrigated are hand watering, underground sprinklers, and drip irrigation delivered through tubing on the soil surface. Choose a single method or use different options in different areas. An irrigation consultant could help you make a plan.

Hand watering. You may decide to water by hand if your yard is small, you live in an area with heavy summer rainfall, or you have native plantings and only a few pots to water. Otherwise it can quickly become tedious.

Underground sprinklers. For large, thirsty areas such as lawns or big sections of uniform plantings, an underground sprinkler system can be a joy, but it must be planned carefully and can't be changed easily. Sprinkler systems require adequate water pressure and flow rates (you may need a booster pump for upslope rotor sprinklers). And installing one requires digging trenches (you can rent a trenching machine). If you choose a sprinkler system for a hillside, use heads with low delivery rates to help prevent runoff. For installation guidance, see the Sunset book *Sprinklers & Drip Systems*.

Drip irrigation. Because it applies water much more slowly than conventional sprinklers, drip irrigation is the common choice for hillside gardens. Drip systems are more accepting of low water pressure or flow rates than underground systems, and they're easier to change. The only downside is maintenance—components tend to get chewed by dogs or damaged by tools. Suppliers of drip components can help you plan an efficient layout for your yard. General guidance is offered here.

Planning a Drip System

Whether you are thinking of a single line of drip tubing or a multicircuit system, a little planning is called for before you roll it out. If all the plants have roughly the same water needs and your garden is small, a single circuit can handle your entire drip system. Otherwise you'll need at least one circuit per hydrozone (see left). Four common drip solutions are illustrated below and on the facing page.

HYDROZONES

By organizing your garden into "hydrozones"—groups of plants with similar watering needs—you can simplify irrigation while giving plants just the amount of water they need. To reduce runoff, locate high-water-use plantings such as lawn, vegetables, and annual flowers on flat or only slightly sloping ground.

CONTAINERS

A length of ¹/₄-inch tubing with an emitter runs from ¹/₂-inch tubing to each container. Treat containers as a separate hydrozone, since they should be watered frequently for just 2 to 5 minutes to keep the soil moist. In large pots, use multiple emitters about 6 inches apart.

SHRUBS

Spirals of ¹/₂-inch tubing encircle shrubs; emitters were inserted directly into the tubing for each shrub. Apply water to just beyond the drip line (where rainfall drips off the edge of the plant canopy).

For sloping areas, run a main drip line downhill and tee off it with separate tubing runs rather than weave a single line back and forth across the hillside. Choose pressure-compensating emitters placed on the uphill side of your plants (gravity will pull the water downhill to plant roots).

If your faucet is at the top of the slope, water will gain pressure as it runs downhill, so a 20-psi (rather than 25 to 30) pressure regulator is recommended as part of the faucet head assembly. If your faucet is at the bottom, suppliers often recommend running a line of supply tubing to the top, placing an air-relief valve there and organizing runs of tubing downhill from that point.

Drip irrigation brings water to diverse plantings across these terraces. When the plants mature, the tubing at left will be hidden. You can also cover drip tubing with mulch.

ROWS OF VEGETABLES

Parallel lines of ½-inch emitter line (with factory-installed emitters, regularly spaced) run along vegetable rows, 16 inches apart. For wider-spaced rows or for a flower bed, use solid tubing with a single emitter per plant (with different flow rates if some plants need more water than others).

LARGE AREAS

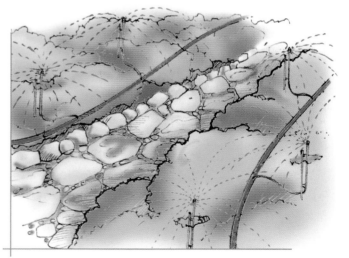

Drip sprayers attached to stakes irrigate an expanse of tall ground cover. Drip sprayers may also be suitable for large beds of flowers that don't mind having their leaves and blossoms wet; use flat-head sprayers to send water out rather than up, and run them early in the morning so plants will be dry by midday. Drip sprayers require more pressure and put out more water than drip emitters, so they have to be on a different circuit.

PLANTING ON SLOPES

UNLESS YOUR HILLSIDE HAS BEEN CONVERTED INTO LEVEL PLANTING AREAS BY MEANS OF TERRACES AND RETAINING WALLS, you'll be growing at least some plants on an incline. On a gentle slope you can plant as if you were on flat ground, but on a moderate or steep slope you must take special care to prevent soil erosion.

ABOVE: Garden chores are more difficult on sloping land than on the flat; for example, you may have to work without a wheelbarrow. Keep maintenance requirements in mind when choosing plants, and design little gardening paths across the slope.

Choosing Plants

Select plants with strong root systems adapted to life on the slant. You'll find some suitable choices in this chapter; check with a local nursery for additional plants that will succeed in your area. Look for low-maintenance species if you want to avoid scrambling around your hillside frequently to weed and prune. On a steep slope, for example, consider a mix of low, spreading shrubs that will grow well with minimal pruning.

In any garden, it's tempting to start off with large plants to make an immediate impact, but young plants in small containers tend to transplant better. Plants in 4-inch or 1-gallon pots make particularly good sense on hillsides where the soil is rocky, shallow, or hard to dig, because the planting holes can be small.

Planting Tips

Before you plant, amend less-than-ideal soil by working in organic matter—if you can. On many slopes, including steep or rocky ones, you may not have much soil to work with, or the soil may slide downhill when you loosen it. In that case, you should disturb the soil as little as possible.

Planting may be similarly difficult. Excavating individual plant pockets just big enough to accommodate the roots is easier than trying to till the soil, and it will interfere less with the slope. You may want to build a basin or terrace around each plant to help retain water (see page 141).

Shrubs and ground covers that require good drainage may rot if water pools around their crowns (where the roots and the stems meet). Set such plants high, and make watering basins behind them; see the illustration above right.

For good coverage, arrange plants in drifts and groves, staggering rows to prevent water from running in a straight line downhill. When planting vines to cover a bare slope, train some of the stems to grow up the slope for more uniform coverage; pin them in place with U-shaped stakes.

Mulching

After planting, apply a thick layer of organic mulch, taking care not to cover plant crowns. Mulch serves many purposes: it keeps the soil from being compacted by heavy rainfall, reduces runoff by slowing down the flow of water, conserves soil moisture so plants can go longer between watering, protects plant roots from excessive heat and cold, and suppresses the growth of weeds.

Organic mulches such as shredded bark, pine needles, and homemade compost also improve the soil. They break down gradually, adding nutrients as they decompose; replenish them periodically. Choose an organic mulch that will stay put on your slope; avoid very lightweight materials such as straw, which tend to blow away, and rounded ones such as some bark chips, which may roll downhill.

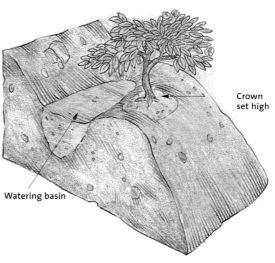

Crown set high

Watering basin

Hold It!

For help in holding soil, plants, and mulch in place until roots develop, use jute netting. Unfurl rolls of the material across the slope, tamp it against the soil, and secure it with the pins sold with the netting. Then cut small, X-shaped holes through which to set your plants in the ground. If you are seeding a hillside, do so before laying the jute.

You don't have to remove jute—it starts disintegrating in a few months—but keep it firmly pinned down while plants are getting started or the soil may erode beneath it.

PLANTS FOR EROSION CONTROL

ON A STEEP HILLSIDE OR A SLOPE WHERE THERE ARE ALREADY SIGNS OF EROSION, CHOOSE PLANTS WITH dense or wide-spreading roots that will knit the soil together and keep it from slipping. The foliage will also protect the soil by dissipating the force of rainfall. Arrange plants in staggered rows to hinder the flow of runoff and help prevent washes from forming.

The strong-rooted shrubs and ground covers listed here will cope with less-than-ideal conditions, such as shallow or poor soil, and provide good-looking cover.

OPPOSITE: Shrubs with striking forms protect and decorate this slope.

Shrubs/Woody Perennials

Artemisia 'Powis Castle'

Woody perennial. Hardy to –20°F/–29°C. Full sun. Little to moderate water. A silvery, lacy mound of foliage to 3 feet tall and 6 feet wide provides a splendid background for the bright flowers of other plants.

California buckwheat
Eriogonum fasciculatum

Shrubby perennial. Hardy to 15°F/–9°C. Full sun. Little to moderate water. This California native, growing to 3 feet high and 4 feet across, has clusters of white or pinkish flowers from late spring to early fall, attracting butterflies; birds enjoy the seeds.

Catalina perfume, evergreen currant
Ribes viburnifolium

Evergreen shrub. Hardy to 15°F/–9°C. Full sun, partial shade in hot climates. Needs no irrigation but can take moderate water; good under native oaks where watering is undesirable. The plant grows to 3 to 6 feet tall and to 12 feet wide, with arching or half-trailing wine red stems. Light pink to purplish flowers from midwinter into spring are followed by red berries. Leathery dark green leaves are fragrant after rain or when crushed.

Forsythia

Firethorn
Pyracantha

Evergreen shrub. Hardiness varies. Full sun. Moderate water. Known for their bright berries, glossy foliage, and fast vigorous growth, firethorns vary in habit from upright to sprawling, in height from 2 to 12 feet. Small spring flowers are a dull, creamy white, carried in flattish clusters; they are profuse, with a scent some people find unpleasant. The real glory of firethorns is their clusters of orange-red berries. Several species and many hybrids are available, some without thorns.

Forsythia

Deciduous shrub. Hardy to –20°F/–29°C. Full sun. Moderate to regular water. From late winter to early spring, the bare, arching branches are covered with yellow flowers. The rest of the year, the medium green foliage blends well with other background shrubs. Many species and hybrids are available, some 8 feet tall, some dwarf.

'Alba' Ramanas rose

Ramanas rose
Rosa rugosa

Deciduous shrub. Hardy everywhere. Full sun or light shade. Little or regular water. Extremely tough, this plant withstands wind, aridity, and salt spray. Wonderfully fragrant roses 3 to 4 inches across range in the many varieties from single flowers to double, from pure white and creamy yellow through pink to deep purplish red. Spring, summer, and early fall blooms are followed by bright red tomato-shaped hips.

Snowberry
Symphoricarpos

Deciduous shrub. Hardiness and light needs vary. Little to moderate water. Upright to arching, typically 2 to 6 feet high and wide, these North American native shrubs spread by root suckers. Clusters of small pink or white flowers in spring or early summer are followed by attractive round berrylike fruit (white or red depending on species) that remains on the branches after leaves drop in fall, attracting birds.

Manzanita
Arctostaphylos

Evergreen shrub. Hardiness varies. Full sun or light shade. Little to moderate water. This enormous clan of plants, native to the Far West, varies from creeping ground covers to treelike shrubs; all have small, urn-shaped white or pink flowers, usually in late winter to early spring. Berries follow, attracting birds. Most manzanitas are characterized by beautiful crooked branches with smooth red to purple bark.

Rockrose
Cistus

Evergreen shrub. Hardy to 15°F/–9°C. Full sun. Little or no water. This sun-loving, fast-growing Mediterranean native is tolerant of harsh conditions—cold ocean winds, desert heat, aridity. A profusion of showy flowers blooms from spring into early summer, sometimes sporadically at other times also, amid soft green, silver, or grayish foliage. Of the many varieties, some reach 6 feet tall, others less than 3 feet.

'Victor Reiter' rockrose

Great Flowering Vines for Slopes

These vines can colonize a slope—just watch that they do not become rampant. Train some stems to grow up the slope for more uniform coverage; pin in place with U-shaped stakes.

Bougainvillea

Cape honeysuckle *(Tecoma capensis)*

Carolina jessamine *(Gelsemium sempervirens)*

Cat's claw, yellow trumpet vine *(Macfadyena unguis-cati)*

Japanese honeysuckle *(Lonicera japonica)*

Lace vine *(Fallopia baldschuanica)*

Passion vine *(Passiflora)*

Star jasmine *(Trachelospermum)*

Rose *(Rosa multiflora, R. wichuraiana)*

Sweet autumn clematis *(Clematis terniflora)*

Clockwise from top: 'Miss Manila' bougainvillea, 'Blush Rambler' rose, Japanese honeysuckle

Ground Covers

Bearberry, kinnikinnick
Arctostaphylos uva-ursi

Evergreen. Hardy to –50°F/–46°C. Full sun or partial shade. Little to moderate water. A dense, foot-high foliage mat spreads at a moderate rate, ultimately covering a wide area and offering a neat appearance all year. Bright green leaves turn red in fall or winter; white or pink flowers are followed by pealike fruits, pink to bright red.

Coprosma × kirkii

Evergreen. Hardy to –20°F/–7°C. Full sun, partial shade in hot areas. Little to regular water; tolerates coastal winds and salt spray. Nearly prostrate or 1 to 3 feet tall, to 6 feet wide, with small, glossy yellow-green leaves, closely set on stems, and red-speckled white berries. 'Variegata' has white-edged gray-green leaves and translucent white berries and grows to 2 feet tall and 5 feet wide.

Cotoneaster, prostrate types

Deciduous and evergreen varieties. Hardiness varies. Full sun. Little to moderate water. Rugged and undemanding, cotoneasters are always tidy, and in spring they bear clusters of white or pale pink blossoms like wild roses. Pea-size fruits follow, turning brilliant red in fall and hanging on well into winter.

Rockspray cotoneaster

Creeping mahonia
Mahonia repens

Evergreen. Hardy to –20°F/–29°C. Full sun or partial shade. Little or no water. Growing to 3 feet tall and spreading by underground stems, this shrub has leaves that are formed of 3 to 7 rounded, dull bluish green leaflets; they take on a reddish bronze cast in winter. Showy clusters of yellow flowers at branch tips in spring are followed by blue berries.

Creeping St. Johnswort
Hypericum calycinum

Evergreen to semi-evergreen. Hardy to –20°F/–29°C. Full sun, partial shade in hot climates. Moderate to regular water. This fast-growing shrub, to 1 foot tall, spreads by vigorous underground stems. Bright yellow flowers resembling single roses bloom throughout the summer.

ABOVE: Ivy (next page) clothes walls and ground with glossy evergreen foliage.

Rosea ice plant (facing page) forms mats of pink flowers alongside a path.

Fragrant sumac
Rhus aromatica 'Gro-Low'

Deciduous. Hardy to −35°F/−37°C. Full sun. Little to moderate water. Growing 2 to 3 feet high, 6 to 8 feet wide, this plant has three-leafleted leaves (to 3 inches long), fragrant when touched or crushed. They turn brilliant red in fall. Tiny yellowish spring flowers are followed by small red fruits that attract birds.

Ivy
Hedera

Evergreen. Hardiness varies. Full sun, some shade in hot climates. Moderate to regular water. Ivy roots densely and deeply. Perfect on slopes, but it can climb walls, fences, and trees. When it is well established, shear or even mow it back to ground level in early spring. Trim regularly in small spaces. English ivy *(H. helix)* is best known, hardy to −15°F/−26°C; 'Baltica' is the hardiest variety, to −20°F/−29°C. The many varieties offer a range of leaf shapes and color variegation.

'Gold Dust' ivy

Juniper, prostrate types
Juniperus

Evergreen. Hardiness varies. Full sun, partial shade in hot climates. Little (or none) to regular water. These widely grown conifers with berrylike "cones" include many ground cover varieties, ranging in height from a few inches to a few feet, in leaf color from greens to silvery blue, gray, and creamy yellow.

'Blue Carpet' juniper

Lantana, prostrate types

Evergreen. Hardy to 25°F/−4°C. Full sun. Moderate water. This fast-growing tropical American native is valued for its profuse clusters of tiny flowers over a long season—all year in frost-free areas. Colors in the many varieties include pink, lilac, white, purple, yellow, orange, and red; many offer a mix of two or more colors.

Lantana

'Maculata' periwinkle

Periwinkle
Vinca

Evergreen. Hardiness varies. Partial or full shade, sun in cool climates only. Little to moderate water. Lavender blue, pinwheel-shaped flowers bloom in early spring among shiny, dark green leaves. Trailing stems root where they touch soil. *V. major,* hardy to 0°F/–18°C, larger and more aggressive, grows to 2 feet tall. *V. minor,* hardy to –30°F/–34°C, is just 6 inches tall. Some varieties have variegated leaves, others white flowers.

Rosea ice plant
Drosanthemum floribundum

Succulent perennial. Hardy to 25°F/–4°C. Full sun. Little to moderate water. A low-growing plant with thick, powdery gray leaves, it

'Yankee Point' wild lilac

makes a 6-inch-high mat, spreading fast. In late spring, its daisylike blossoms create a solid sheet of cool, shimmering pale pink that attracts bees.

Rosemary, prostrate types
Rosmarinus officinalis

Evergreen. Hardy to 10°F/–12°C. Full sun. Little to moderate water. Needlelike leaves are pungently scented, and small blue blossoms from fall into spring attract birds and bees. Stems root as they spread, so that one plant becomes a colony. If grown atop a wall, stems will trail down in waterfall fashion. 'Huntington Carpet' ('Huntington Blue'), popular as a ground cover, has pale blue flowers, grows to 1½ feet tall, and spreads quickly yet maintains a dense center.

Wild lilac, prostrate types
Ceanothus

Evergreen. Hardiness varies. Full sun. Little to moderate water. This large-scale ground cover—some varieties grow to more than 15 feet across—has dense, dark green foliage with clusters of blue flowers that appear in early spring.

Great Grasses for Erosion Control

Grasses hold hillside soil in place with fibrous roots or creeping rhizomes. For quick results, consider seeding your slope with low-growing annual grasses such as ryegrass and brome.

Alkali sacaton *(Sporobolus airoides)*

Big bluestem *(Andropogon gerardii)*

Bull grass *(Muhlenbergia emersleyi)*

Deer grass *(Muhlenbergia rigens)*

Foothill needle grass *(Nassella lepida)*

Little bluestem *(Schizachyrium scoparium)*

Nodding needle grass *(Nassella cernua)*

Side-oats grama *(Bouteloua curtipendula)*

Switch grass *(Panicum virgatum)*

Wild rye *(Leymus condensatus)*

Big bluestem

PLANTS FOR A ROCK GARDEN

ABOVE: A rock garden weaves stone and plants into a vibrant hillside tapestry.

HILLSIDES, ESPECIALLY THOSE THAT HAVE BOULDERS, ARE NATURAL SETTINGS FOR ROCK GARDENS. THE BEST-LOOKING rock gardens are generally composed of compact plants that make tidy mounds or spreading mats. Plant the most drought-tolerant species near the top of your slope or mound, the ones that need more water lower down. If you choose true alpine plants, remember that they are used to a tough life. Water infrequently but deeply, and do not over-fertilize.

Alpine columbine
Aquilegia alpina

Perennial. Hardy everywhere. Full sun to light shade. Regular water. Above lacy foliage on slender stems growing to 2 feet tall rise beautifully poised bright blue flowers, which are very attractive to hummingbirds.

Aster

Perennial. Hardiness varies. Full sun. Regular water. Many low-growing types are suitable for a rock garden. *A. alpinus,* hardy to −30°F/−34°C, develops a 6- to 12-inch-tall tufty mound, with violet blue flowers late spring to early summer. *A. × frikartii* (−20°F/−29°C)

has open, spreading growth to 2 feet high with abundant lavender to violet blue flowers in early summer to fall. *A. tongolensis* 'Napsbury' (−10°F/−23°C) produces summer flowers of dark blue with orange centers, rising on 6-inch stems from tufts of dark green leaves.

Heath
Erica carnea

Evergreen shrub. Hardy to −10°F/−23°C. Full sun except in hottest climates. Consistent, careful watering. Needs excellent drainage; tolerates neutral or slightly alkaline soil. Upright branchlets rise 6 to 16 inches from prostrate main branches. In winter and spring, rosy red flowers bloom among small, needlelike medium-green leaves. Prune every year to keep heath handsome.

Aubrieta
Aubrieta deltoidea, A. × cultorum

Perennial. Hardy to −5°F/−21°C. Full sun or light shade. Needs water before and during bloom. A low, spreading mat of gray-green foliage forms to 6 inches high and 1½ feet across. Numerous tiny flowers are deep red, pale to deep lilac, or purple.

Basket-of-gold
Aurinia saxatilis

Perennial. Hardy to −30°F/−34°C. Full sun or light shade. Moderate water. Self-sows readily. Dense clusters of tiny golden yellow flowers in spring and early summer rise from gray leaves on stems 8 to 12 inches tall. 'Citrina' ('Lutea') has pale yellow flowers, 'Sunnyborder Apricot' apricot-shaded ones.

Cheddar pink
Dianthus gratianopolitanus

Perennial. Hardy to −30°F/−34°C. Full sun, but some afternoon shade in hot areas. Regular water. Very fragrant flowers, typically pink to rose, open on stems 6 to 10 inches high from neat mounds of blue-gray to green-gray foliage, blooming from spring to fall if spent flowers are clipped.

Coral bells
Heuchera sanguinea

Perennial. Hardy everywhere. Light shade, full sun in cooler climates. Regular water. Leaves with scalloped edges form a compact evergreen clump. Wiry stems 1 to 2½ feet tall bear clusters of dainty, bell-shaped bright red or coral flowers. Heucherella hybrids combine the flowering habit of coral bells with the heart-shaped leaves of foamflower (*Tiarella cordifolia*).

Dwarf Alberta spruce
Picea glauca albertiana 'Conica'

Evergreen shrub. Hardy to −30°F/−34°C. Full sun or light shade. Little to moderate water; needs shelter from drying winds and strong reflected sunlight. Compact and cone-shaped, this shrub takes 35 years to reach 6 to 8 feet tall and 4 to 5 feet wide.

Gypsophila repens

Perennial. Hardy to −40°F/−40°C. Full sun. Moderate water. Small white or pink flowers bloom in clusters on trailing 1½-foot stems. Overall height is 6 to 9 inches.

'Royal Blue' aubrieta

Planting a Rock Garden

With your plants still in their pots, experiment with placing them. Once you like the arrangement, begin planting. Set plants deep enough that the top of each root ball is about ½ inch above the soil. Then spread crushed gravel over the entire rock garden, including a little around the crown of each plant. Water well.

Houseleek
Sempervivum

Succulent perennial. Hardy to –20°F/–29°C. Full sun, light shade in hottest climates. Little to regular water; needs good drainage. Tightly packed leaf rosettes produce little offsets around the parent rosette. The many species include easy-to-grow *S. tectorum* (hen and chickens), with gray-green rosettes, red or reddish flowers.

Lewisia

Perennial. Hardy everywhere. Full sun or light shade. Little to moderate water. These Western natives boast extremely showy flowers. Bitterroot *(L. rediviva),* Montana's state flower, has 2-inch spring flowers that look like water lilies. *L cotyledon,* from Oregon and Northern California, has smaller flowers from spring to early summer. Both need excellent drainage.

Mexican daisy
Erigeron karvinskianus

Perennial. Hardy to –5°F/–21°C. Full sun or light shade. Moderate water. A graceful trailing plant to 20 inches high, with multitudes of white-pink daisylike flowers from early summer into fall, Mexican daisy is invasive unless controlled. 'Moerheimii' is more compact, with lavender-tinted flowers.

Sedum

Succulent perennial. Hardiness varies. Full sun or partial shade. Little to moderate water. Many small types of these plants, varying greatly in form, are nice for rock gardens. *S. brevifolium,* 10°F/–12°C, is a tiny (to 3 inches high), slowly spreading plant with red-flushed gray-white leaves and pinkish or white summer flowers. *S. spathulifolium* forms rosettes of $^{1}/_{2}$- to 1-inch spoon-shaped leaves on short, trailing stems.

Sedum

Yellow-blooming sulfur flower is a native of western mountains, growing at the timberline and above.

Snow-in-summer

Snow-in-summer
Cerastium tomentosum

Perennial (short-lived). Hardy to −20°F/−29°C. Full sun, partial shade in hot areas. Regular water; needs good drainage. Dense, spreading, tufty mats of silvery gray leaves, to 8 inches high, showcase masses of white flowers in early summer.

Stonecress
Aethionema

Perennial. Hardy to −20°F/−29°C. Full sun. Little to moderate water; grows best in light, porous soil with considerable lime. These choice little plants produce long clusters of pink flowers on spiky stems in late spring to summer; deadhead spent blossoms for best bloom. *A. × warleyense* (*A.* 'Warley Rose') is a neat, compact hybrid, to 8 inches high, that is planted widely in warmer climates. *A. schistosum*, to 10 inches high, has slate blue leaves and fragrant, rose-colored flowers.

Sulfur flower
Eriogonum umbellatum

Shrubby perennial. Hardy everywhere. Full sun. Little to moderate water. Low, broad mats of woody stems with feltlike leaves carry late spring or early summer clusters of tiny yellow flowers that age to rust.

Sunrose
Helianthemum nummularium

Evergreen shrub. Hardy to −20°F/−29°C. Full sun. Moderate water. Surefire color is provided from midspring through early summer by flowers ranging from bright red to pastel pink or white. Plants grow to 8 inches tall and 3 feet wide.

Planting a Wall

Most of the thousands of rock-garden plant species grow readily in dry-laid stone walls. Plant your wall as you build it. After laying each course of stones, line the largest gaps with sphagnum moss. Fill the pockets with soil (whichever type each plant prefers), set the plant roots into the soil, tamp the soil in place, and water gently.

Thyme
Thymus

Shrubby perennial. Hardiness varies. Full sun, partial shade in hot areas. Moderate water. Heavily scented leaves and masses of little flowers in late spring or summer are attractive to bees. Creeping thyme, *T. serpyllum* (−10°F/−23°C), reaches 6 inches high, with dark green leaves and small purplish white flowers in summer. Woolly thyme, *T. pseudolanuginosus* (0°F/−18°C), reaches 3 inches high, with small, woolly gray leaves.

Trailing phlox
Phlox nivalis

Perennial. Hardy to −10°F/−23°C. Full sun or light shade. Regular water. A trailing plant to 6 inches high and a foot wide bears pink or white flowers in fairly large clusters in late spring or early summer.

Trailing phlox

Wall rockcress

Wall rockcress
Arabis caucasica

Perennial. Hardy to −20°F/−29°C. Full sun, with some shade in hot climates. Moderate water. A dependable old favorite for stone walls and rock gardens, wall rockcress forms a mat of gray leaves to 6 inches high, almost covered with white flowers in early spring.

WATER GARDENING

SEVERAL DIFFERENT KINDS OF PLANTS WILL GROW IN A POND. SOME FLOAT FREELY ON THE SURFACE, unrooted in soil. Others, notably water lilies, are rooted in pots placed deep in the water; their leaves float on the water surface. Marginal plants such as iris—found in nature at stream or pond edges, in 1 to 6 inches of water—are rooted in submerged pots but rise up above the water. And then there are oxygenating plants, those dark green ferny waterweeds that grow entirely underwater and help keep the water clean.

TYPES OF AQUATIC PLANTS
When you look at plantings in a pond, you may not at first realize that they are set at different levels in the water. To accommodate individual depth requirements, place plants on marginal shelves or on clean bricks, concrete blocks, flat rocks, or inverted plastic pots.

Marginal plant Free-floating plant Marginal plant raised in pond Marginal plant Deep-water plant Oxygenator

FREE-FLOATERS
Add a free-floating plant such as a water hyacinth to a pond or water pot simply by launching it onto the surface of the water.

Free-Floating Plants

The roots of free-floaters dangle in the water, absorbing nutrients directly from it. Their leaves and flowers, shifting and swaying in a breeze, add movement to a pond or a large water pot, but they can quickly cover the entire water surface. In mild-winter regions, certain kinds are banned because they are invasive, endangering natural lakes and rivers. Even if they are legal in your area, thin your free-floaters regularly or you'll lose sight of the water.

Deep-Water Plants

Plants that grow with their leaves floating on the surface and their roots underneath in pots—like water lilies and floating heart—are called deep-water plants (sometimes floating-leaf plants or semi-floaters). They thrive in calm water away from the splash of waterfalls and fountains.

Water lilies are the most widely grown plants in this category. Easiest for beginners to grow are the hardy types, which bloom in flushes throughout warm weather, go dormant in fall, and can overwinter in a deep pond.

Louisiana irises (shown here with white spider lilies), available in a wide range of colors, thrive at pond and stream margins.

Tropical water lilies start to bloom a little later in summer than hardy varieties, but their bloom season extends longer—often until the first frost. Their blooms are generally larger, more fragrant, and more numerous than those of the hardy lilies. Although tropical lilies go dormant in winter, they should be brought indoors in all but the mildest climates. They grow best when outdoor temperatures are above 70°F/21°C, so they shouldn't be set out again too early in the growing season.

Lily containers can be fairly shallow but should be wide—around 20 inches wide and 10 inches deep for large varieties, half those dimensions for miniatures. Place slow-release fertilizer tablets in the soil near the bottom of the pot. Plant the lily so its crown is exposed above the gravel layer on top of the soil.

SOIL FOR AQUATICS

You can leave an aquatic plant right in its nursery pot if there is room for the roots to grow. If you need to repot, use garden soil. The best type is a heavy soil free of peat moss, manure, or other amendments that might float away or pollute the water. If your soil isn't suitable, you can buy an aquatic mix. After planting, add a 1-inch layer of gravel on top to hold the soil in place.

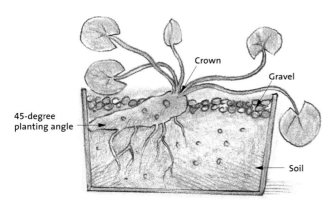

HARDY WATER LILY
Hardy water lilies grow horizontally. Fill the pot partway with soil, then set the lily against the inside edge with the growing point angling upward about 45 degrees toward the center. Add soil to within 2 inches of the top and then add a layer of gravel.

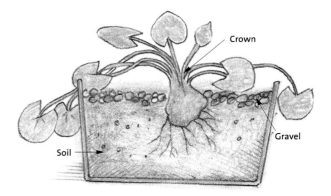

TROPICAL WATER LILY
Plant a tropical water lily upright in the center of a pot that is nearly filled with soil, then add a layer of gravel.

PLANTING MARGINALS

A marginal in a 4-inch pot is being transplanted with a second plant into a larger pot made of porous, rot-resistant fabric. Many types of pots can be used—plastic mesh baskets, for example—but fabric pouches don't need lining, they conform to the surface on which they are placed, and they have no sharp edges to harm fish.

Marginal Plants

Most aquatic plants are marginals. They like to grow in the shallows, with their foliage in the air and their roots submerged in water as deep as 6 inches, depending on the variety. Plant one to a pot, or more than one in a large pot, using heavy garden soil or an aquatic soil mix—but no fertilizer. Place the pot in the pond on a shelf or a pedestal of some kind (see page 156).

You can also plant marginals in trenches on a stream edge; see the illustration on page 126. Be sure to cover the soil with gravel and pebbles so it won't leak into the stream. If your stream doesn't have a trench, you can create a planting area behind a rock dam, as shown at right. The landscape fabric behind the dam helps prevent the soil from passing into the stream.

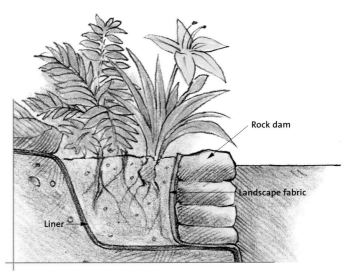

Rock dam

Landscape fabric

Liner

Great Aquatic Plants

FREE-FLOATERS

Water hyacinth *(Eichhornia crassipes)*

Water lettuce *(Pistia stratiotes)*

DEEP-WATER/FLOATING-LEAF PLANTS

Floating heart *(Nymphaea peltata)*

Parrot feather *(Myriophylum aquaticum)*

Water lily, hardy type *(Nymphaea)*

Water lily, tropical type *(Nymphaea)*

MARGINALS

Canna hybrids

Japanese iris *(Iris ensata)*

Lotus *(Nelumbo)*

Taro, elephant's ear *(Colocasia esculenta)*

Water hyacinth

Oxygenating Plants

Oxygenating plants grow entirely underwater, like the water-weeds in natural streams. Add a few of them to your pond or water pot and you'll have less algae—oxygenators absorb the nutrients in water, starving out algae.

The aquarium sections of pet stores are good sources of oxygenators. Two common ones are Canadian pondweed (*Elodea canadensis*) and eel grass (*Vallisneria americana*). Plant a bunch in a small pot of gravel and place it on the bottom of the pond.

Adding Fish

Mosquito fish and the less exotic types of goldfish are the easiest fish to keep in a water garden. To acclimate your fish when you bring them home from the store in a plastic bag, float the bag on the water for about 20 minutes before releasing the fish. Use a cloth to keep the bag shaded from hot sunlight.

There's no need to feed pond fish, but if you do, be sparing—extra fish waste will encourage algae growth. Besides providing life and movement, fish contribute to a water garden's ecological balance by eating mosquito eggs and algae.

Keeping the Water Clear

Algae is a vigorous water plant; it will thrive when abundant warmth, light, and nutrients are available. To contain its growth without resorting to algicides (which don't prevent algae from returning immediately), keep the water as free of nutrients as you can. That means keeping fish waste and leached plant fertilizer to a minimum and removing plant debris before it decomposes.

Having plants in the water, especially large-leafed or spreading floating plants, reduces the light available for algae growth. Plants also use nutrients in the water, leaving less for algae. Oxygenating plants absorb nutrients especially efficiently, making them an important element in a strategy to combat algae. Fish can help, too, since they feed on algae.

If you do decide to use an algicide, be sure to check the product's effect on wildlife.

COMBATING MOSQUITOES

To keep mosquito larvae from hatching in the water, let fish feed on them or add a small amount of the biological control *B. t. israelensis* (available in donut rounds called "mosquito dunks").

The blossoms of tropical water lilies stand above the water.

INDEX

Page numbers in **boldface** type refer to photograph captions.